THE CHOCOLATE CHRONICLES

RAY BROEKEL

Some of the material in this book has appeared in slightly different form in *Candy Wholesaler*, *Chocolate News*, and *Candy Bar Gazebo*.

The Enjoyable Diet, pages 86-91, reprinted courtesy of the National Confectioners Association.

BAKER'S is a registered trademark of General Foods Corporation. Recipes, pages 78-81, reprinted with permission of General Foods Corporation for their nostalgic value only.

Recipes, pages 83-85, reprinted courtesy of the Nestlé Company, Inc.

Cover Photograph by Perry L. Struse, Jr. Photographed at The Valley Junction General Store through the courtesy of Betty Veiock, Proprietor.
Cover Design and Layout: Heather Miller
Make Up: Mary Jane Strouf
All Other Photography: Ray Broekel

ISBN 0-87069-431-6

Library of Congress Catalog
Card Number 84-051257

10 9 8 7 6 5 4 3 2 1

Copyright © 1985

Ray Broekel

published by

Wallace-Homestead Book Company
580 Water's Edge Road
Lombard, Illinois 60148

One of the *ABC PUBLISHING* abc *Companies*

For Peg and Fergus, who assisted in
research on many a candy bar.

Acknowledgments

A special thanks to all those who helped make this book a reality.

And a very special thanks to Sheila Albert, Allen Allured, Norm Anderson, Isaac Asimov, Rita Atalanta, Tom Aylesworth.

Patty Wolcott Berger, Don Biron, Alan Bitterman, Annabelle Black, Malcolm Blue, Ben Bova, William E. Boyer, Jim Boyle, Lora Brody, Art Buchwald, Robert Burkinshaw.

Gary Carney, Mary Blount Christian, Beverly Cleary, Dawn Dahl, Tomie dePaola, Iris Edwards, Nancy Elmont, Dick Ely, Ed Emberley, Bob Feller, R. Widden Ganong, Amanda Gaw, Hollis Gerris, Dale Glade, Shelley Grossman.

Barry Halper, Collin B. Hamer, Jr., Wes Johnson, Robert Johonnot, Don Jones, Robert J. Harrington, Robert Hayden, Mark Heidelberger, Nicholas Herb, Thomas Hodge, Craig Hoffman, Jim Holmes, Dorothy B. Hughes.

Leonard Kallok, Susak Kamke, Kathy Kelly, Harold Kenyon, Herb Knechtel, J. L. Kretchmer.

Jennie Lee, Dean Leibson, Nancy Levin, Elizabeth Linington, Lew Lipset.

John D. MacDonald, William Manchester, Madeline Manetta, Adrianne Marcus, John Martin, Clayton Martoccio, Don Martoccio, Neal Maxfield, Vard Maxfield, Fred McCarthy, Greg Mcdonald, Alix Mendes, Glen Milnor, Ned E. Mitchell, Bill Mobley, Ben Myerson.

Joan Lowry Nixon, Dick O'Connell, Edmond Opler, Ruth Patterson, George Pearson, Elise Piazza, Charles R. Pihringer, Gloria Pitzer, Bill Pronzini.

William E. Reid, Chloe Ramacier, J. C. Ramsden, Gloria Maria Rando, Seymour Reit, Jak Ritchie, Verne N. Rockcastle.

Les Sass, Bill Schuler, Bill Sherman, Morris Sloan, Jimmy Spradley, Austin Starr, David Starr, Bill Start, Marian Stearns, David Stivers, Marie-Claude Stockl, Roy Sugden, Jack Sweet.

Diane Terwilliger, Jack Thompson, Paul Udelle, John Updike, Rudy Vallée, Donald Wakeman, Ramona and Jay Ward, Lawrence Welk, Donald Westlake, Phyllis A. Whitney, Phil Williams, Bill Yantis, and Milt Zelman.

My apologies to those individuals I overlooked. Editorial judgment has been used in establishing dates and other data where discrepancies occurred in reference sources.

Last of all, thanks to all the great folks at Wallace-Homestead.

Contents

Preface

During the Depression, a penny bought quite a bit—especially if you were a kid with a few coppers burning a hole in your pocket. Then, mouth watering and legs pumping, you ran all the way to the neighborhood Mom and Pop store to splurge on penny candy.

Would you buy bull's-eyes, Mary Janes, banana squares, nonpariels, candy corn, or eggs filled with fancy cream or marshmallow?

Or would you pick Walnettos, malted milk balls, caramels, licorice pipes or rats, orange slices, or spearmint leaves? Jaw-breakers, cinnamon hots, licorice whips, mint lozenges, rock candy, or moth balls? Boston baked beans, BB bats, or sugar men?

Or taffy with peanut butter, molasses kisses, jujubes, teddy bears, horehound drops, one-cent Baby Ruth bars, one-cent Tootsie Rolls, one-cent Butterfingers, or one-cent Hershey bars? Or dabs of sugar candy on waxed paper, fireballs, coconut squares, fudge squares, or peppermint sticks?

The candy counter promised all of these plus much more. How could you possibly make up your mind with an assortment like this to choose from?

Slowly you deliberated, while "Mom" or "Pop," holding a little, white, empty paper bag almost went to sleep behind the counter.

Finally, momentous decisions made and pennies spent, you left the store clutching your little bag full of penny candies as though it held priceless treasure.

One unforgettable day you became the wealthiest kid on the block, thanks to the benefice of a whole nickel bestowed on you by a favorite aunt, uncle, grandma, or grandpa. Suddenly you were eligible to enter the wondrous world of the five-cent candy bar! And what a choice of sweet delights awaited you then at the candy counter! A candy bar loaded with crunchy nuts, tangy fruits, fluffy nougat, or creamy caramel—chocolate coated or chocolate filled—would be yours for the first time.

The selection was almost limitless. But, fortunately, you were a veteran of many penny candy forays by now. Undaunted, you plopped your nickel on the counter and made your choice. Chances are good that you chose a chocolate candy bar, since most of the candy bars (80 percent) made at that time were either chocolate coated or had some form of chocolate inside them.

You left the shop with a big smile on your face in greedy anticipation of savoring every delectable bite. In *The Chocolate Chronicles*, the stories are flavored with the taste and aroma of that very first candy bar you bought on a day, not so long ago, for only five cents. You'll discover that chocolate remembered can be almost as satisfying as chocolate consumed. But without the calories. Read and enjoy!

Introduction

In the last few years, chocolate has appeared in the news frequently, because of a surge of enthusiasm for it and for the American chocolate bar.

In the first part of this book you'll find stories about how American candy bars got their names, the people who made them, and other sweet bits of trivia from the good old days when they cost just a nickel. You'll also be exposed to a bit of history as we travel around the country chronicling the candy Americans grew up with.

Interested in using candy bars to create special desserts? Part Two will be right down your alley. It starts with the steps in making chocolate and candy bars. For fun we've included great candy bar and candy recipes of the past, plus a selection of delicious new recipes and some that imitate the popular candy bars of today. To put these recipes in proper perspective, Part Two concludes with "The Enjoyable Diet," a most sensible diet that will help you lose weight while eating well-balanced meals and candy to boot!

The final parts of the book contains some delightful revelations from well-known personalities about their favorite candy bars, some tales about kids of the Thirties, and other stories relating to chocolate, candy, people and even a dog named Fergus.

Candyland Histories

Sweet Memories

Remember those candy treats you had when you were a kid? Brings back sweet memories, doesn't it? Now here's a chance to test your memory about confectionery products of the past and present.

1 What is the present best-selling candy bar in the United States?
   a. Mounds
   b. Hershey's Milk Chocolate
   c. Snickers

2 Who made the first peanut bar back in 1906?
   a. Squirrel Brand
   b. Planters
   c. Mr. Goodbar

3 What candy bar had a wrapper picturing a roasted chicken on a plate when it first came out in the 1920s?
   a. Cold Turkey
   b. Baby Lobster
   c. Chicken Dinner

4 What candy bar, no longer being made, was named after a baseball player?
   a. Baby Ruth
   b. Reggie!
   c. Pecan Pete

5 Which candy treat was named after a favorite aunt?
   a. Tootsie Roll
   b. Mandy
   c. Mary Jane

6 Which of the following candy bars sold in a quarter-pound size for five cents in the 1930s: Baby Ruth, Butterfinger, or PowerHouse?
   a. the first two
   b. only Butterfinger
   c. all three

7 What was the first candy bar Frank Mars made?
   a. Mar-O-Bar
   b. Ping
   c. Forever Yours

8 What famous radio comedy team had a candy bar named after it in the 1930s?
   a. Laurel and Hardy
   b. Stoopnagle and Budd
   c. Amos and Andy

9 What is the name of the dog shown on the Cracker Jack box?
   a. Lassie
   b. Bingo
   c. Nipper

10 Admiral Byrd took two-and-a-half tons of candy on his trek to the South Pole. What kind was it?
   a. Necco Wafers
   b. Nestlé Milk Chocolate
   c. Charleston Chews

11 In what business did Milton S. Hershey first become a millionaire?
   a. making marshmallows
   b. making chocolates
   c. making caramels

12 Which of the following candy bars was not named after a popular dance?
   a. Tango
   b. Zag Nut
   c. Dipsy Doodle

13 Which of the following is not a caramel sucker?
   a. Sugar Daddy
   b. Whiz
   c. Slo Poke

14 What candy bar was introduced to the public through a sky-writing campaign?
   a. Sky Bar
   b. Clark Bar
   c. Almond Joy

15 What giant in the candy industry failed several times before making a go of it in the confectionery business?
   a. Frank Martocchio
   b. Frank Mars
   c. Peter Paul Halajian

16 Which national landmark had a candy bar named after it?
   a. Yellowstone Park
   b. Old Faithful
   c. Death Valley

17 In 1926, a booklet came out with recipes for using a candy bar in salads, desserts, and tea-time dainties. The candy bar was:
   a. Bonomo's Turkish Taffy
   b. Old Nick
   c. Oh Henry!

18 Which of the following chocolate companies, all well known for their cocoa, made commercial chocolate bars for a period of time?
   a. Runkel Brothers
   b. Walter Baker and Company, Inc.
   c. both of the above

19 A German immigrant who was in the brewery business turned to a sweeter business of confections when Indian arrows were shot into his dining room. He was:
   a. Mr. Schuler
   b. Mr. Schrafft
   c. Mr. Brach

20 Daniel Peters joined forces with what other Swiss compatriot to come up with the formula for making milk chocolate?
   a. Dieter Streisvogel
   b. Johann Bachoffen
   c. Henri Nestlé

Answers:

1. c	6. c	11. c	16. b
2. a	7. a	12. b	17. c
3. c	8. c	13. b	18. c
4. b	9. b	14. a	19. a
5. c	10. a	15. b	20. c

Bar to Barr

It was at the Chicago World's Columbian Exposition in 1893 that the first mass-produced American chocolate bar became a twinkling in the eye of Milton S. Hershey. The Exposition celebrated the anniversary of Christopher Columbus's arrival in the New World in 1492. But because of inclement weather that delayed completion, the fair opened a year late. When it did open in 1893, there were many surprises for those in attendance.

Most of the visitors to this world's fair enjoyed their first exposure to Thomas Edison's electric lights. Buildings and fountains bedecked with Edison's invention bathed the entire exposition with light during the dark hours. Another of the marvels at the exposition was the world's first Ferris wheel. The big wheel had been developed by George Washington Ferris. The thirty-six cars on it each held around sixty passengers, and the entire wheel was twenty-six stories high!

Courtesy Norman Anderson

Chocolate-making machinery from Dresden, Germany, was on display at the exposition. When Milton S. Hershey saw the machinery, he immediately decided to invest in the chocolate business to supplement his already successful caramel business. By 1894, he began turning out on a limited scale the first mass-produced chocolate bars in the United States. But it wasn't until World War I that chocolate bars really caught the public's fancy. That's when commercial marketing began in earnest, not only for Hershey, but for other confectioners as well.

Another gentleman at the Columbian Exposition in 1893 was Walter M. Lowney. He'd begun in the candy business in Boston in 1880. He experimented with making chocolate bars and was probably the first to produce hand-made chocolate bars in the United States. He exhibited his bars at the exposition and received favorable comments about his product.

No one from Canada exhibited any chocolate products at the exposition, but by 1910 Arthur Ganong came up with the five-cent Chocolate Nut Bar, a Canadian first. He and a factory superintendent had made the bars at the Ganong Candy Company in St. Stephen, New Brunswick, to take along on a fishing trip.

Not all confectioners in attendance at the Columbian Exposition were interested in chocolate. One gentleman hawking his wares was Frederick William Rueckheim. He was busily selling his popular popcorn-peanuts-molasses confection, which three years later was christened Cracker Jack.

One of the biggest hits of that world's fair had nothing to do with candy, but was one of the midway shows. The Street of Cairo featured Fahreda Mahzar Spyropolos. She was better known as Little Egypt and introduced the hootchy-kootchy, or belly dance, to the American public. Her appearance made the fair a success, as people flocked to see her, lured by the barker's oratory:

> When Little Egypt dances,
> every fiber and every tissue in
> her whole anatomy shakes like
> a jar of jelly from your grand-
> mother's cupboard. She's hot,
> red-hot, gentlemen. Enjoy the
> experience of a lifetime for just
> ten cents!

After a lapse of about fifty years, another world's fair was held in Chicago. Opening in May, 1933, it was called the Century of Progress International Exposition. A feature of that fair was the Sky Ride. Two steel observation towers, each 625 feet high, were connected by cables over which ran "rocket cars" carrying passengers. The towers were 1,850 feet, or about one-third of a mile, apart. Passengers could view the fair below—a most colorful sight in the evening when all the bright lights were flashing.

Courtesy Alan Bitterman

The Beich Candy Company capitalized on this aspect of the fair by coming out with a Sky Ride Candy Bar. The blue, red, and yellow wrapper had a drawing of the observation towers and the skyways, complete with passenger cars. The bar sold well during the fair, but disappeared after the fair closed.

The Century of Progress also had a mid-way. This one also featured a street show, but the city name was switched from Cairo to Paris. And at The Streets of Paris, Helen Gould Beck, better known as Sally Rand, performed her dance with two ostrich fans, flicking them about dexterously to reveal brief glimpses of her white powder-coated body. Because her show was always jammed with customers, her beginning salary of $15 a week was raised to $3,000 by the end of the summer.

Chocolate and other candy items were always big sellers at shows of any kind—especially at burlesque shows, where candy butchers came out between the acts to cajole the audience into buying boxes containing a few bits of confectionery products and a so-called "big prize" that seldom existed. Burlesque shows featuring comedy sketches began about 1865. And about 1920, the strip-tease became the top attraction in burlesque, while comedians took up the slack. Such performers as Fannie Brice, W. C. Fields, Phil Silvers, and Al Jolson started their careers in burlesque.

Some of the strippers who developed the striptease to a high degree of professionalism were Ann Corio, Gypsy Rose Lee, Margie Hart, Georgia Southern, Sherry Britton, Faith Bacon, and Lili St. Cyr.

It wasn't long before some of the peelers took on trick names, such as Apple Pie, the All-American Dish; Peppy Cola; Bonnie Bell; Ann Tenna; and Alky Seltzer, the Bumps and Burps Girl.

Perhaps the best known of the trick-name performers was one who starred on a street that's always an exposition—Bourbon Street in New Orleans. Her name was Juanita Dale Phillips. In the late 1950s, at the height of her career, she quickened the pulse of many a young man out on the town. An attractive woman, Juanita came up with the trick name, Candy Barr. She never billed herself as such, but she could have called herself The First Great American Candy Barr.

Chances are are that Milton S. Hershey and Juanita Dale Phillips never met nor had any business connections over the years. But they did have one thing in common—they both launched their careers capitalizing on one word, "bar." Milton spelled his with just one r, while Juanita used two.

Small world.

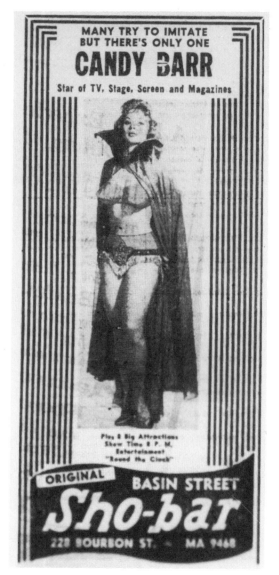

MANY TRY TO IMITATE
BUT THERE'S ONLY ONE
CANDY BARR
Star of TV, Stage, Screen and Magazines

Plus 8 Big Attractions
Show Time 8 P. M.
Entertainment
"Round the Clock"

ORIGINAL BASIN STREET
Sho-bar
228 BOURBON ST. • MA 9468

Believe It or Not

In the 1920s and early 1930s, few candy companies distributed their products nationwide. To compete with those who did (such as Curtiss and Williamson), smaller companies used various gimmicks. One such gimmick was to make use of a nationally recognized name. Another was to form a loose combine of companies to blanket the nation with sales. Each member of the combine had certain market areas in the country.

In 1931, four companies created one combine. The Bradley Smith Company of New Haven, Connecticut, covered New England and New York City. Minter Brothers of Philadelphia had New York State, Pennsylvania, New Jersey, Delaware, Maryland, D.C., and Virginia. Walter Johnson Candy Company of Chicago (with a factory in Los Angeles) sold in the Midwest, West, and South. And Imperial Candy Company of Seattle covered the Pacific Northwest. Under contract, the combine called one of their candy bars, as Ripley says, "Believe It or Not!"

All Set!
...on the Biggest
Merchandising Event
in Candy Bar History

THE tie-up with Ripley's popular illustration features, appearing in over two hundred newspapers from coast to coast, gives this new "Believe It or Not" bar immediate acceptance over a national area. Its quality, together with the merchandising plan back of it, will keep this bar moving.

5c
Packed 24s

Shipments will be made with the first touch of fall weather. In the meantime, get your order on file with one of the manufacturers below serving your territory:

The BRADLEY SMITH CO.
NEW HAVEN, CONN.
for New England and
New York City zone

MINTER BROTHERS
PHILADELPHIA, PA.
for New York State, Penns'l'va, New Jersey, Delaware, Maryland, D. C., Va.

WALTER JOHNSON CANDY CO.
341 W. SUPERIOR ST., CHICAGO
for Central West and Southern States

IMPERIAL
CANDY CO.
SEATTLE, WASH.

☐ "BELIEVE IT OR NOT! we are willing to take a chance on .... cartons—enough for once over to our retail accounts; Ship us your first release on this new bar.
☐ Send samples and wholesale prices on BELIEVE IT OR NOT.

NAME ....
ADDRESS ....

Reprinted from The Confectionery Buyer, 1931, courtesy The Manufacturing Confectioner

In 1932, Robert Ripley's popular illustrated features were appearing in more than two hundred newspapers from coast to coast. Ripley started his feature of the strange and bizarre in 1918, and it was first syndicated in 1929. In the 1930s "Believe It or Not!" was at the height of its popularity.

Ripley had been a sports artist for the old *New York Globe*. On a fateful day in 1918, he was looking around for an idea to tie together his daily sports cartoons. Nothing clicked. In desperation, he gathered some sports oddities from his scrapbook and files. One of the numerous items in the first cartoon was a man who walked across the continent backwards, using a mirror for better vision. Ripley finally settled on the title, "Believe It or Not!" The rest is history, as the feature eventually appeared in more than three hundred newspapers in thirty-eight countries and in seventeen languages.

Ripley became a world traveler, always searching for the unusual. He became a famous radio personality, and his first museum, Odditorium, drew crowds at Chicago's Century of Progress Exposition in 1933. Ripley's work appeared in many books and later on TV. And today, Ripley International, Ltd., continues promoting that which Ripley brought into the world.

Ripley died in 1949, but he outlived the candy bar that carried his logo. It enjoyed a few years of success in the candyland marketplace in the 1930s, but soon found a more permanent home in Candyland Cemetery, where so many name bars have found their final resting place.

Let's Hear It For the Chicken

The biggest chicken around today is probably the San Diego Chicken, who performs during the baseball season. But in candyland, the big chicken was the Chicken Dinner candy bar manufactured by the Sperry Candy Company.

Courtesy Alan Bitterman

Courtesy Alan Bitterman

Chicken Dinner was one of the early nut-roll bars and first came out in the early 1920s. The first Chicken Dinner wrappers pictured a whole roasted chicken sitting on a dinner plate. In the years following World War I, the economy made many families feel fortunate if they had one good meal a day on the dinner table. A whole roasted chicken on a candy bar wrapper symbolized something substantial in terms of food value.

To help promote Chicken Dinner, Sperry decorated a fleet of Model-A Ford trucks with eye-catching sheet-metal bodies built to resemble chickens. Eventually, the Sperry people learned that a chicken didn't quite convey a candy bar image, so the bird was dropped from the wrapper. The name, however, continued.

Courtesy Charles Phringer

The image of a chicken as the symbol of a good meal goes back to Henry IV, King of France (1589-1610), and is attributed to his coronation speech. "I hope to make France so prosperous," he said, "that every peasant will have a chicken in his pot on Sunday." Centuries later, the 1932 Republican campaign capitalized on the slogan, "A chicken in every pot."

Sperry Candy Company was founded in the early 1920s by Fred Foster, a wholesaler of candies and fountain supplies, and Miles Sperry and Ray Pihringer, who had been in the restaurant business in Elkhorn, Wisconsin. They began making candies of different kinds as a sideline to their restaurant business, and they developed some potential five-cent candy bars. A manufacturing plant was built in Milwaukee next to the wholesale business run by Fred Foster (Barg and Foster).

Next to Chicken Dinner, the most successful Sperry bar was the Denver Sandwich, which had a wafer between candy layers. Sperry produced many other bars over the years, including Fat Emma, made in the early 1930s, Straight Eight, Pair o'

Kings, White Swan, Chicken Spanish, Club Sandwich, Cool Breeze, Big Shot, Hot Fudge-Nut, Prom Queen, and Cherry Delight. Coming along later were such bars as Coco-Mallow, Coco Fudge, Cold Turkey, Almond Freeze, Mint Glow, Koko Krunch, and Ripple.

Ray Pihringer and two former associates started a new company, The Chocolate House, in 1945. In 1962, the Pearson Candy Company of Minneapolis bought Sperry and closed the Milwaukee plant. Sperry products were then made in the Minneapolis factory. By 1967, Sperry was again sold, this time to Schuler Candy Company of Winona, Minnesota, and bar production was called to a halt. Such old favorites as Denver Sandwich and Chicken Dinner were retired for good.

What a shame that Chicken Dinner's gone. It was a good-tasting bar. And wouldn't it be great to see a big fleet of those Chicken Dinner Model-A Ford trucks still zipping down the highway?

When All America Listened

Perhaps the most popular radio show ever broadcast was the "Amos 'n' Andy" program. In the early 1930s, movie house marquees announced that at seven o'clock, the film would be stopped so the "Amos 'n' Andy" radio program could be piped in. The listening audience probably numbered more than forty million a night when the program began its peak in 1931. Everyone from Herbert Hoover to J. Edgar Hoover, Fanny Brice to Al Capone, tuned in six nights a week to the program, which was fifteen minutes long in its early years.

Amos was Freeman F. Gosden, and Charles J. Correll played Andy. They used black dialect to portray their characters. The program first aired in 1928 in Chicago and ran until the 1950s. A TV version was launched in 1951, but lasted only until 1953. Since Gosden and Correll were white, black actors played the roles on TV. "The Amos 'n' Andy" show came to a close in the 1950s. Because of the emerging civil rights movement, it was considered no longer appropriate to the times.

Like others in the early candy bar business, George Williamson of Chicago's Williamson Candy Company looked for bar names that were immediately recognized by the public. So when the "Amos 'n' Andy" radio show became a hit, Williamson arranged with Charles Correll and Freeman Gosden to produce an Amos 'n' Andy candy bar in 1930. The bar had a crisp honeycomb center and was chocolate covered. It sold reasonably well for only a few years before dropping by the wayside.

George Williamson had latched onto

another big name a few years before the Amos 'n' Andy bar. Reaching into the world of politics, he came up with the name Alfred Emmanuel Smith. This resulted in the Big Hearted Al candy bar, a chocolate-coated marshmallow confection.

Al Smith, who was dubbed the Happy Warrior by his protegé, Franklin D. Roosevelt, was the 1928 Democratic candidate for president. Smith's popularity, like that of his namesake candy bar, Big Hearted Al, quickly lost its foothold in the marketplace when Smith was defeated for the presidency by Herbert Hoover. Big Hearted Al lost its space on candy counters to bars with more winning names.

George Williamson tried many times to come up with another winner comparable to his successful Oh Henry! bar. Around 1921, that bar carried a sub-logo on wrappers showing a woman in a kitchen with the words, "Aunty May's." At the time, the bar sold for ten cents. The Aunty May sub-logo was soon dropped.

Zowie!
He's Shot Another Goal!

He's a winner, that boy! Yes, sir! He's got the pep! And pep is what makes winners! Pep! Energy! Being just a fraction of a second faster than the other fellow.

Candy is the best little pep-maker that you ever ate. That's why the big college players get a mouthful of candy during the games. It makes quick energy! But it must be pure candy. KNOW the candy you eat.

Oh Henry! is just as pure as if your mother made it at home. Nuts, sugar, milk, chocolate . . . fine, pure foods! And the purest grades that can be bought. It's just full of ENERGY! Try a bar.

Know Your Candy!

Oh Henry!
Eat it for ENERGY! 10c

Sometime, try the new candy the Oh Henry! people are making, called "COPY of Oh Henry!" . . .

REMEMBER that candy is a food . . . wouldn't you rather know that your candy is made with rich, *full cream* milk instead of skim milk? . . . with plump, crisp nut meats . . . with chocolate that belongs in dollar-a-pound boxes? The trifle more Oh Henry! costs is your assurance of such quality.

Taste the difference yourself!

Know Your Candy

A *convenient portion* of dollar candy!

Oh Henry!

Try the new 5c candy made by the Oh Henry! people . . . "Copy of Oh Henry!" . . . the finest candy ever made for 5c.

Basketball Hero 2 Point JIM — Eats Oh Henry! — to keep in trim

Everybody's Candy Bar!

Oh Henry! 5¢

"CALL TIME OUT" the Goalie cried — Ate Oh Henry! — Turned the tide

Everybody's Candy Bar!

Oh Henry! 5¢

Double Dipt Oh Henry! 5¢ Covered with Pure Milk Chocolate

This $1.75 BASEBALL for Only 69¢ and 7 Oh Henry! Wrappers – ALL CHARGES PREPAID

Some Williamson bars of the 1920s and early 1930s were Oh Oh, Long Distance, Choice Bits, Big Alarm, Copy, and That's Mine. With the exception of the Big Alarm bar, they all contained peanuts—apparently Williamson's favorite nut. All those bars were hand wrapped, as they were produced before the days of automated wrapping machines.

17

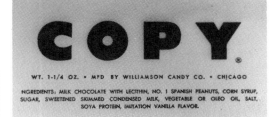

Several new Williamson bars made their appearance in the 1950s. The Oh Mabel! bar was known as Oh Henry!'s little sister candy bar. It did a bit better in the market than Oh Henry!'s first sister bar, Fat Emma, in the 1920s. Oh Mabel! contained toasted coconut, among other ingredients.

Attributed to George Williamson's Scottish influence was the Laddie bar, a butterscotch-flavored nut roll. Williamson's earlier Salted Nut Roll appeared again in the 1950s under the name Oh Nuts!. It was introduced to retailers as a three-bar bonus offer in regular boxes of twenty-four-count Oh Henry! bars. Oh Nuts! wasn't around long. Maybe Williamson muttered, "Oh, nuts!" at its demise. Introduced in the late 1950s or early 1960s was Choc-O-Nuts!, a chocolate flavored nut roll. That bar appeared in various weights.

Williamson's Salted Nut Roll, which sold for five cents, was a combination of fudge, caramel, and peanuts. It was an Oh Henry! without the chocolate covering. Another popular Williamson item in the late 1920s and 1930s was the novelty item Guess What?. It came in a box and contained four candy kisses plus a surprise toy. The back of each box showed a puzzle or cutouts.

Courtesy Don Jones

Williamson made a few departures from the basic nut roll. One item, Choc-O-Mint, was a good chocolate-covered mint, but it didn't sell well in the late 1950s and early 1960s.

Also in the 1960s were several versions of the sweet/sour candies that were becoming popular. The first version was labeled Sour N' Sweet, but the name was soon changed to Papeete Punch. The last name change was to Popins. That candy came out in 1964, the same year as the movie *Mary Poppins*. The movie did well, but the candy bar didn't, and the line was soon dropped.

Courtesy Don Jones

Courtesy Don Jones

The best seller, of course, has been the Oh Henry!, produced for more than sixty years. During that time, it has appeared in many weights, including a one-pound bar. That bar got a nice bit of free publicity one year when Buddy Hackett showed it on "The Tonight Show" with Johnny Carson.

Advertising campaigns for Oh Henry! were numerous and effective. When John Dillinger was rampaging throughout the Midwest in the 1930s, he was the FBI's first officially designated Public Enemy Number One. It wasn't until a number of years later, however, that the term was adopted in Oh Henry! advertising, which declared the bar to be "Public Energy Number One!" This great play on words was the theme for an effective advertising campaign.

When Henry "Hank" Aaron was the home-run champ of the National League, he appeared in numerous TV commercials for Oh Henry!. And over the years, numerous Oh Henry! Easter eggs were produced as a seasonal item. They were good five- and ten-cent sellers for several years.

Now manufactured by Nestlé, Oh Henry!, George Williamson's contribution to the honor roll of classic candy bars, should continue to flourish on the market.

Put and Take

Today's games of chance include state lotteries, in which the big cash prizes can be around a million bucks, give or take a few thousand clams. And, of course, there are the legalized forms of gambling run in the state of Nevada and in Atlantic City, New Jersey.

In comparison, yesterday's games of chance, such as punchboards, seem pretty tame in terms of the money either risked or won. Punchboards could be found almost anywhere you looked—Mom and Pop stores, cigar stores, cafés, taverns, drugstores, pool halls, grocery stores, service stations, and variety stores.

Punchboards first appeared in the early 1900s and grew steadily as a business for decades. By 1951, the industry was considered a billion-dollar business or racket, depending on how you looked at it.

Punchboards were self-contained games of chance. A board was made of pressed paper and had several holes that contained coded tickets. A player paid an agreed amount, then used a key punch to extract the ticket. Prizes were awarded to winning tickets.

In most areas of the country, punchboards were viewed merely as trade stimulators involving small change, so law enforcers left storekeepers alone. At first the awards were cash, but soon cigarettes, toys, watches, cameras, and pens were offered as prizes. Merchants found this an effective way of moving some of their products, and merchandise prizes removed the appearance of blatant gambling. Thus, the wheels of prohibiting legislation were halted for many years.

There were numerous candy companies, especially in the 1920s and 1930s, that produced candy bars specifically for the punchboard market. The Belmont Candy Company of Memphis, Tennessee, issued the 1-Two-3 Bar. The Push 'em Up Tony Bar was produced by Dietz Candy Company of Milwaukee, and the Fitger Candy Company of Duluth, Minnesota, had a

1¢2¢3¢ bar. The Walter H. Johnson Candy Company, Chicago/New York, made Brown Beauty and CrOwK bars. And One Two Three came from Jefferson Candy Company of Chicago/New York.

Candy bars and other candy items were popular punchboard prizes for many years. Some boards gave away a piece of candy with each punch. One kind, called the Put and Take, required the player to put up from one to five cents for each punch, and take a designated number of candy bars.

Sparklers was made by Magic City Candy Company in Birmingham, Alabama. Hollywood Candy Company made several punchboard candy bar specials. You Bet was made by Overland Candy Corporation of Chicago, and the Good Luck bar came from the Queen Anne Candy Company in Hammond, Indiana.

21

Another kind of punchboard cost one cent per punch. If a player had a ticket ending in five or zero, he won a free candy bar. The last punch on the board earned five candy bars.

As in any game of chance, odds were generally against the player. Today, the punchboard is history, since the law now frowns on its use.

Sherlock Holmes and the Case of the Many Fat Emmas

In the early 1920s, The Pendergast Candy Company in the Minneapolis/St. Paul area was quite active as a confectioner, and Pendergast candy makers were trying to come up with a formula for a new candy bar with a chewy nougat center. The candy makers goofed with the formula, however, by adding too much egg albumen. The result was not a chewy nougat, but a new kind of fluffy, airy, puffy nougat. Thus was inadvertently born the candy bar center that became known as the Minnesota Nougat or Minneapolis Nougat.

The Pendergast Candy Company decided to market its new bar under a new name. The name chosen for the bar before the formula goof was Emma. But because of the larger size created by the fluffiness, the adjective "fat" was tacked on to create Fat Emma.

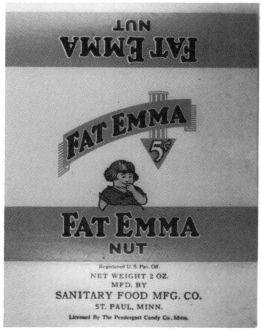

Other candy makers quickly realized the potential in the new type of nougat and came up with their own version of the Pendergast formula. Frank Mars (in Minneapolis at the time) introduced his Milky Way and other fluffy nougat-center bars. Fenn Brothers, Inc., of Sioux Falls, South Dakota, produced Walnut Crush. Two Walnut Hill bars were made—one by the Redel Candy Corporation of Milwaukee in the 1920s and 1930s, and the other by Candymasters Inc. of Minneapolis in the 1940s.

Pendergast Candy Company at one time made the Fat Emma as a quarter-pound bar, but they quickly found the bar to be too expensive to manufacture and market. Consequently the Pendergast Company stopped making the bar, but they did license the name to other companies. One of those companies was the Sanitary Food Company of St. Paul. Sanitary made a two-ounce Fat Emma for a short time.

Another licensee in the 1920s was George Williamson, one of the most respected confectioners in Chicago. Buoyed by the success of his Oh Henry! candy bar, Williamson decided to launch another bar—this time one bearing the name of a female counterpart to Oh Henry!. Williamson decided to latch onto Fat Emma which Pendergast was then licensing.

The public relations firm in Chicago that handled the Williamson's business assigned a recent Chicago high school graduate to the account. The young miss was trim and attractive, and she disliked

the name Fat Emma. But since the account was her first job, and the name had been okayed by the president of the candy company, the young miss pitched in to do the best she could in the advertising campaign. The buying public, though, didn't cotton to the bar's name either. So the Williamson Fat Emma bar slid into oblivion after about a year of mediocre sales.

On December 27, 1928, the Pendergast Candy Company was purchased by the F. A. Martoccio Macaroni Company of Minneapolis and became part of its candy division. A variation of the Fat Emma formula was already being produced by Martoccio (later Hollywood Candy Company) under its Double Milk Shake name. Now Martoccio had the Fat Emma name and made the bar for a short time using peanuts and a divinity nougat center.

After Hollywood moved to Centralia, Illinois, the modified formula again appeared in a bar. Walnuts were substituted for peanuts in the Smooth Sailin bar. It sold well right into the 1950s before being phased out.

In the early 1930s, a Fat Emma bar was produced for a while by the Sperry Candy Company of Milwaukee. And in the years 1937–1939, the name Fat Emma surfaced north of the border. During those years, McCormicks Ltd., London, Ontario, sold a Fat Emma. It was a 4" x 4" x 1" marshmallow bar coated with chocolate. According to one source, Fat Emma bars were available in Canada about ten years ago, but they're no longer on the scene.

The formula was a goof, but the result was a real success. Fluffy nougat centers became popular in numerous candy bars. Had Pendergast stuck with just Emma rather than Fat Emma, who knows what might have resulted? To paraphrase Sherlock Holmes, "It's elementary, my dear Watson, that you be careful when using adjectives."

Of Fig Bars and Fig Pies

About halfway between Chicago and Milwaukee lies a town where the bakery Fig Bars and candy Fig Pies were born. The town of Zion was officially launched in 1900 after a year of planning and surveying by John Alexander Dowie.

Dowie was a Christian zealot who moved to Chicago in 1893. By 1896, his Christian Catholic Apostolic Church had acquired a large following. Dowie, an advocate of "clean living," began to look for land on which to build a city where his followers could live under the laws of his church.

He chose 6,400 acres of farmland between Chicago and Milwaukee, where Zion grew almost overnight. Strict laws enforced by Dowie and his church controlled all activities. The Church owned all industrial and commercial establishments. Theatres and drugstores were prohibited, as were sales of liquor, tobacco, playing cards, oysters and clams, rabbit meat, and pork.

Completed in four months in 1901, a large all-frame structure housed male members who came ahead of their families to build homes in the new city. The

building had more than 350 rooms and in later years was known as the Zion Hotel. It became a Midwest landmark before being razed in 1979. Buildings to house the various industries controlled by the church were also hurriedly constructed. By the early 1900s, about twenty industries governed by the church as Zion Industries, Inc., had taken shape.

Two of those industries were the Baking Division and a Candy Division. The Baking Division first produced a general line of crackers, cookies, cakes, and pies. But soon church leaders were seeking a distinctive product. They looked to the Bible and therein found reference to the fig. And so was born, in 1920, the Zion Fig Bar, a product that was to make the name Zion a household word throughout much of the United States, especially from the 1920s through the 1950s.

The Candy Division first turned out a general line of candy, and by the 1920s was producing candy bars. Due to the popularity of the Baking Division's Zion Fig Bar, the Candy Division introduced its own version—the Fig Pie. It was a chocolate-coated candy bar with a confectionery center. Other candy bars that were good sellers in the late 1920s and into the 1930s were the Cheer Leader, Cocoaroon, and Cherry Sundae.

Courtesy Alan Bitterman

Wilbur Glenn Voliva, who oversaw the church after Dowie's death in 1907, strictly enforced the law established by Dowie. But by 1939, Voliva lost political control of the city, which had alternated between prosperity and bankruptcy over the years. Through reorganization, the real estate was allotted to individual owners. Today Zion resembles its neighboring communities and differs little from mainstream America. A main attraction of the community each April and May is the Zion Passion Play, which was first performed in 1935.

The Baking Division is the only division of Zion Industries still in operation. The Candy Division closed in 1961. The Zion Fig Pie sold well into the 1940s and early 1950s before disappearing. It deserves a place in candy bar history if for nothing else than that it was inspired by verses in the Bible.

Brother's Three, Plus Two

In 1909, the Pearson Candy Company of Minneapolis was incorporated by P. Edward Pearson and his brothers Oscar and John. The three were soon joined by two other brothers, Waldemar and Fritz. The first Pearson Nut Goodies were produced in 1912. By 1927, the company devoted its efforts to producing five-cent candy bars.

Courtesy George Pearson

During the 1920s, the Pearson company not only sold its own products, but also those of many other confectionery companies. Other companies' products then shared the pages in the Pearson sales catalog. They included several Planters products—Jumbo P-Nuts 5¢, Self Starter, 1918 Bar, Planters 5¢ Nutty Bar, and Planters Milk Chocolate Peanut Bar. Beich's Milk Chocolate Almond Nougat and Chocolate Nut Bar were listed, as was Whitman's Cream Cocoanut Bar. Pictures of all the bars accompanied the catalog listing.

Courtesy George Pearson

Mackenzie's of Cleveland listed their Scotch Lassies and Old Hickory bars. Also from Cleveland were Glick's Tom and Jerry and Glick's Mellow Whip.

From Allen Qualley of Minneapolis came the Cherry High Ball. Others were Lyon's Chocolate Cream Cakes, Popous Bars from Phelps, Chocolate Cream Cocoanut bars from Webers, Sommer-Richardson's Chocolate-Covered Pineapple Bar, Bardall's Coco Rula, Blue Seal Nougat Bar, Kratchwil's Nut Rolls, Blue Bell Nut Creams, Wan-eta Lunch, Dickenson's Maple Confection, and Redel's Yacki-Hula.

Unwrapped bars featured in the catalog included Mackenzie's Old Hickory (available both with and without wrappers), Blue Bell Tee Dee, Big Eater, Blue Bell Pecanola, Filbert Bar, Repeater Bar, and King Sol, just to name a few.

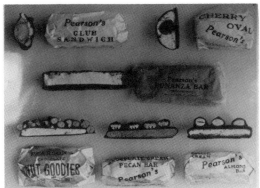

Some wrapped Pearson bars featured were Club Sandwich, Bonanza Bar, Pecan Bar, Almond Bar, The New Recruit, Peanut Square, Marshmallow Bar, Cherry Oval, and, of course, Nut Goodies.

Pearson's Salted Nut Roll (now known as Peanut Nut Roll) was first produced in 1933 at the height of the Great Depression. By World War II, only five Pearson bars were still being produced: Nut Goodies, Salted Nut Roll, Log Cabin Fudge, Cherry Dipper, and Pecan Roll. For a time, the Salted Nut Roll was wrapped under the Choo Choo label, since rival manufacturers were making similar bars and using the Salted Nut Roll name. Later Choo Choo was dropped and Pearson's name was prominently displayed.

In 1951, Pearson bought Trudeau Candies, Inc., of St. Paul and took over such famous Trudeau bars as Seven Up, Variety, Mellow Square, and Mint Pattie. In 1962, Pearson bought Sperry Candy Com-

27

pany of Milwaukee, and in 1967 sold it to Schuler of Winona, Minnesota. Pearson made several of the Sperry bars, including Chicken Dinner and Denver Sandwich, while it still owned that company.

In the 1960s, Pearson made its own mint and packaged it in a DeMets Mint wrapper, a Marriot Hot Shoppes Mint wrapper, and a Fred Harvey Mint wrapper.

Fred Harvey was a phenomenon of his time. He opened his first Fred Harvey restaurant in 1876 in the Santa Fe depot in Topeka, Kansas. More of his restaurants were soon opened along the Santa Fe line and in other depots, and eventually Harvey opened hotels along with his restaurants. The restaurants all shared the high Harvey standards and were staffed by the well-trained Harvey Girls, who were hired by the hundreds and sent West. The eminent wit and sage Will Rogers was to later observe that Fred Harvey "kept the West in food and wives."

Fred Harvey died in 1901, but his business enterprises continued for many more years. In the 1960s, one of the featured items in Harvey restaurants was the Fred Harvey Mint made by Pearson.

Other Pearson bars of past years that are no longer made include Brazil Gems, Pecan Caramel, Cluster-ette, Fore Bar, As You Like It, Creme De Menthe, Summertime, Golden Fluff Marshmallow, Log Cabin Divinity, My Sweetie, Coconut Fudge, and the "By George" candy bar.

The Pearson Candy Company, St. Paul,

Minnesota, now owned by Ronald Cappadocia, continues to roll merrily along producing confectionery products of merit. So be it, thanks to the original brothers three, plus two.

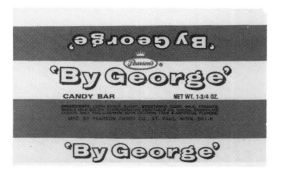

Martoccio's Macaroni Factory and the Hollywood Connection

The F.A. Martoccio Macaroni Company, Inc., was organized in Minneapolis, Minnesota, in 1911. In 1922, Frank "Marty" Martoccio bought the Pratt and Langhof Candy Company. He made the purchase when a motor burned out in his macaroni factory and he went to Pratt to buy a motor advertised for sale. The owner of the candy business, which was temporarily shut down, convinced Marty to buy him out by promising to make the candy and teach Marty the business.

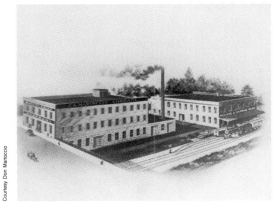

Courtesy Don Martoccio

In 1928, the assets of the Pendergast Candy Company, also of Minneapolis, were purchased. That company, creator of the Minnesota Nougat, was already making numerous candy bars. Production was immediately augmented with a new bar called Milk Shake. It had a chocolate-flavored nougat center and was topped by caramel and covered in chocolate.

In 1933, son Clayton Martoccio, became manager of the macaroni factory, and Marty devoted full time to the candy business. The company decided to adopt a new corporate name for the various branches of the business, and the name Hollywood Brands, Inc., was chosen. The reason for this choice isn't known, but we can guess that it had to do with Ameri-

ca's romance with the movie industry. Marty undoubtedly reasoned that the buying public would associate star billing and status with the products produced under the Hollywood name.

Clayton Martoccio sold the macaroni factory in 1936, but continued to make candy. Soon a bigger and more centrally located factory was needed. A large former envelope factory in Centralia, Illinois, was offered to the company. In 1938, Hollywood left Minnesota to relocate in Centralia. All the bars already developed in Minneapolis, as well as an ever-increasing line of new bars, created concern about an adequate milk supply. Ultimately, two dairies were purchased, followed by the purchases of a candy factory in Montgomery, Alabama, and a peanut factory in Okmulgee, Oklahoma. The Hollywood Candy Company had its own fleet of about eighty trucks to haul their candy bars to warehouses nationwide for faster distribution.

Around 1940, two employees of Hollywood decided to go into the candy business for themselves. They moved back to Minneapolis to form the Candymasters Company. Two of their bars were Coffee

Dan and North Pole. The name for another of their bars, brought with them from Illinois, was Walnut Hill. Walnut Hill candy bar was named after a small town located about six miles from Centralia. As a twin to that bar, Candymasters produced their Brazil Hill bar, which was made with Brazil nuts rather than walnuts. The Candymasters Company was eventually taken over by F. and F. Laboratories of Chicago and its candy bar line was phased out.

In the 1960s, Hollywood Candy Company was number two in volume of candy bars made. Although national in distribution, many of the Hollywood bars were made specifically for certain regions, where they were then marketed. A division of Hollywood in Ashley, Illinois, the Hoben Candy Corporation produced bars through the late 1960s. They included Dazzle, Picnic, Chills, Chocolate Malted, Hoben's Nut Roll, Hoben's Star Roll, and Pecan Picnic.

According to company records, Hollywood was the first candy company to coat a bar with a synthetic coating. Synthetic coated bars held up much better in hot weather than did milk chocolate-covered bars, so Hollywood got a jump on the candy industry with its new method of coating its Zero bar.

When punchboards were the craze, Hollywood provided its own boards to sell their candy bars. Often the big prize on those punchboards was a candy bar that weighed as much as one pound. Special Hollywood bar wrappers were made for the bars given away with punchboards.

Those punchboard bars included Toffy Nut, Sundae, Tuesday, and Teddy Bear. The Hollywood punch boards were promoted in taverns, cigar and cigarette stores, and various other locations.

Of course, the best-known Hollywood bars were Milk Shake, Pay Day, Zero, and Butter Nut. But over the years, many names appeared under the Hollywood star. Remember Big Pay, Top Star, All Star, Magic, Nut Sundae, Spot Pecan, and Taffy

Nut? Or Big Chief and Hail? Some bars first sold for three cents were Picnic, Dazzle, and Chills. Nickel bars included Chocolate Malted, 3 Big Bears, Big Time, Sno King, and Aero. The bar Red Sails was named after a top tune of 1935, "Red Sails in the Sunset." The bar called Hollywood was a good seller for years. And, of course, there were such popular 10-cent bars as Marty's Toasted Almond, Marty's Walnut, Marty's Pecan, and the popular Smooth Sailin'.

In 1967, the Martoccio family sold Hollywood to Consolidated Foods, Inc., of Chicago. Some of the Martoccio family continued under Consolidated ownership, but eventually they left to follow other pursuits. The Martoccio family, by the way, didn't get back into the macaroni business. But that, of course, is another story.

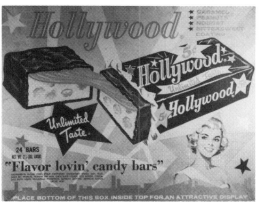

Two Men from Mars

Frank Mars and Milton S. Hershey had two things in common. They became perhaps the two greatest successes in the candy business, and both of them failed numerous times in the candy business before eventually getting on the right track.

Milton S. Hershey had many early failures. He first tried to set up shop in Philadelphia, Chicago, and New York, before finally becoming a success making caramels and chocolate.

Frank Mars also tasted defeat several times before finally striking it rich. In 1902, in Minnesota, he married Ethel G. Kissack. By 1910, she had divorced him and was awarded custody of their son, Forrest.

Frank soon married another Ethel— Ethel V. Healy. Frank had been working as a candy salesman, but now he decided to take his new bride to Seattle and go into the candy business for himself. When that business soon failed, Frank and Ethel moved to Tacoma to open another candy

The Great American Candy Bar Club

Wouldn't one taste
good — *right now!*

Milky Way

Old Candy Ads unmounted - $4.00 to $10.00

business in 1911. One of his competitors was the Oriole Candies Company, which proved too much for Mars, and he filed for bankruptcy.

The West Coast no longer held any promise for Mars, so he took his wife back home to Minnesota. In 1920, the two lived over a one-room factory in Minneapolis. Frank made the candy and Ethel peddled it to retail stores.

Ready cash was a problem for Frank, so he often couldn't order candy ingredients in bulk. Instead, he bought items such as sugar in small lots from other candy makers in the Minneapolis-St. Paul area. At the Pearson Candy Company, orders were left with employees to accept only cash for a one hundred-pound sack of sugar because Frank's credit wasn't too good.

Frank's first name for his company was Mar-O-Bar Company in honor of his first candy bar by the same name. The bar wasn't a success in the marketplace, but Frank kept plugging away. He didn't know it, but his break was soon to come.

One of the more active candy compa-

nies in the Minneapolis-St. Paul area at the time was the Pendergast Candy Company. In the early 1920s, Pendergast created their Minnesota or Minneapolis Nougat (see pages 22, 29).

Other candy companies in the Minneapolis-St. Paul area quickly came up with their own versions of the nougat, because the candy center was most tasty by consumer standards. Frank Mars immediately saw the nougat's potential and, using high-quality ingredients, he created the Milky Way bar in 1923. The bar had a chocolate nougat center (later, for a short period of time, the Milky Way also was available with a vanilla nougat center), and Frank was hoping to cash in. But business got rough again, and Frank leased the rights to make the Milky Way bar to Schuler Chocolates, Inc., of Winona, Minnesota. It wasn't until Frank Mars started his next candy plant, this time in the Chicago area in 1929, that he bought back the Schuler rights to the Milky Way candy bar for five thousand dollars.

Courtesy Bill Shuler

24 Milky Way Bars 24

Schuler MILKY WAY

NET WEIGHT 2¼ OZS. OR MORE

Picturesque home where Milky Way is made in ideal, sunlit kitchens by The Community of Candy Makers. Milky Way tastes so good because every ingredient in it is the finest obtainable. Quality—that is the secret of the Milky Way flavor you crave.

MARS, Inc., 2019-2059 North Oak Park Ave., Chicago, Ill.

Frank's Chicago plant became a success, and he turned on the steam to produce quality candy that quickly caught the public's fancy. For most of his products, he utilized the fluffy nougat center that was to become a Mars hallmark. Bars that prospered over the years were Snickers, 3 Musketeers, and the Mars Bar. Forever Yours was popular for many years but then fell by the wayside. And there were others that enjoyed success for a few years before leaving the marketplace. By 1930, Mars was on his way to becoming one of the leading confectioners in the country. Consumers recognized that Frank was producing quality candy with taste appeal.

Courtesy Leonard Kallok

Frank's son Forrest had spent his formative years on the West Coast with his mother. In his junior year of college he transferred to Yale. After graduation, he joined his father in the newly opened Chicago plant. The two never really saw

33

eye to eye. Both were individualists and perfectionists in their own way. It was in 1932, so the story goes, that Frank gave Forrest fifty thousand dollars, the foreign rights to Milky Way and other Mars bars, and the edict to leave the country to start his own business.

Forrest opened a factory near London. He anglicized the American bars to the British taste, and soon Mars, Ltd., became a leader among confectioners in the United Kingdom. Forrest, like his father, insisted on quality and cleanliness. He soon began to branch out into other food areas, including a company set up to produce food for pets. He also began working on another business that eventually developed into Uncle Ben's Rice, which he parlayed into big business when he returned to the United Sates at the outbreak of World War II.

While in England, Forrest became aware of a popular confectionery item produced by Rowntree and Company, Ltd. Smarties first came out in 1937 and soon caught the public's fancy. They were pellets of chocolate, coated with a hard candy finish in pastel hues. The concept of candy-coating chocolate intrigued Forrest.

When he returned to the United States, he quickly took on a partner, who just happened to be the son of the president of Hershey's. With Bruce Murrie as a partner, Forrest's new company was assured of a good supply of cocoa even during the war years. The two partners combined the initial letters of their last names and christened their company

M&M Ltd. Naturally, their first product was named M&M's. The year was 1941.

Frank Mars only enjoyed a few years of success as a candy man before he died in 1934. Ethel was president of the company until her death in 1945, but the company was run by her half brother, William Kruppenbacher, after Frank's death. Kruppenbacher was responsible for the sponsorship of the popular radio quiz show, Dr. I. Q., first aired in 1939. A candy bar of the same name was a stellar Mars seller for a number of years before being retired.

Upon Ethel's death, Forrest hoped he'd have a chance to run his father's company. Eventually, after years of infighting between a half sister and Kruppenbacher, Forrest gained control of the company. Once that was accomplished, he built it into the largest income-producing confectionery company in the United States.

After Forrest retired to Las Vegas in the mid-1970s, the company, now known as Mars, Inc., continued under the leadership of two sons.

Forrest couldn't stand retirement and became restless. He began experimenting with candy in a small experimental kitchen. Again he zeroed in on ingredients of highest quality, including an ingredient common to gourmet candy in Europe—liqueur centers. After about five years of work, he opened a candy factory in Henderson, Nevada, and named it after his mother, the first Ethel Mars. Unfortunately, she died in Las Vegas at age 97 shortly before the Ethel M Plant opened. The liquor-filled bonbons became an immediate success in Nevada but couldn't be shipped out of the state. Other Ethel M candies, however, soon became a symbol of high quality throughout the country.

So ends the tale of the two men from Mars. Both had drive, ambition, and the will to succeed. They never compromised on quality and they improved on other companies' good ideas. Because of this, Frank and Forrest earned their rightful places in the Candyland Hall of Fame.

On a First-Name Basis

The Old World provided the United States with a wealth of individuals who succeeded in the world of candy. Armenia provided its share of blossoming confectioners, including Deran S. Hintlian. After he arrived in the United States at the age of seventeen, he went to work in his uncle's candy factory.

In 1929, Deran and his brother Karnig acquired the bankrupt Windsor Confectionery Company in Somerville, Massachusetts. Along with another Armenian confectionery compatriot, Peter Paul Halajian, Deran Hintlian decided a last name wasn't necessarily a good business name, so the company was named Deran Confectionery Company, putting it on a first-name basis.

The Hintlians did some manufacturing and jobbing and also ran a retail candy store. Cellophane was a new product at the time, and the Hintlians were among the first to use this product for wrapping candy bars and packing peanuts.

Deran took over the Murray Confectionery Company in Boston in 1931. And in 1936, Deran moved to Cambridge, Massachusetts, where it now operates as part of Borden Confectionery Products. Other candy makers acquired by Deran were Miller and Hollis Corporation and the C. S. Allen Corporation of Webster Massachusetts. The latter plant relocated to Connecticut, where the company still makes its chocolate coatings.

In 1956, a Deran representative came up with the idea of an open-top, multiple "dump display," which would allow customers to serve themselves from a variety of confectionery items. A crude hand-lettered sign that read "Mix-Up Special" and later became "Pick 'n Mix" called attention to the display, which featured all the candy at the same price per pound. The sign was affixed atop this first display in a variety store.

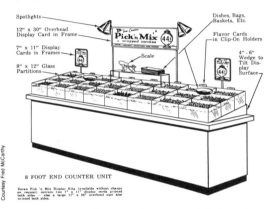

The gimmick proved successful, but it was a few years before the concept really caught on. The Pick 'n Mix idea eventually grew into a multi-million dollar business.

During the 1940s and 1950s, Deran made a number of candy bars. One of those bars was originally titled Maple Pecan, but when pecans became somewhat scarce, the more easily obtained walnuts were substituted, and the bar name was changed to Maple Walnut. Other bars of the time were My Baby, P-X Lunch, Mint Patty, Cocoanut Patty, Wintergreen Patty, and a chocolate-covered marshmallow bar, Good Joe. For a time in the 1980s, a Campfire Marshmallow bar was produced under the Borden Confectionery Products label.

Without a doubt, Deran Hintlian, a standout among confectioners, deserves an honored slot in the Immigrant Confectioners Hall of Fame.

Lolly Pops and Boo-La Boo-La

The word lollypop (also spelled lollipop) was recorded as far back as 1796, when it referred to sweet lozenges (without sticks) purchased by children. Author William Thackeray used the word in his novel, *Vanity Fair*, in 1848. Charles Dickens also used the word in several of his novels.

In the 1850s, what could be called makeshift lollypops appeared in the United States. They differed from the original lozenges in that they were made by putting small dabs of sugar candy on the ends of slate pencils for kids to nibble at.

In the late 1880s a candy merchant named Reynolds of West Haven, Connecticut, got into the act. Mr. Reynolds was manufacturing a chocolate caramel taffy, and to make it easier to eat, he put it on a stick.

One of Mr. Reynold's customers was George Smith of New Haven. Mr. Smith and his partner, Andrew Bradley, manufactured hard candies as the Bradley, Smith Company, founded in 1883.

George Smith thought the stick idea was a great one and, beginning in 1892, utilized it with the hard candies his company produced. The product sold for a while without a name, and it took a race horse to finally suggest one.

Mr. Smith, who enjoyed going to the races, attended the state fair one day to watch the horses run—especially the most popular and outstanding race horse in the East at the time, a horse named Lolly Pop. Lolly Pop's owner had perhaps been influenced by reading one of Dickens's novels, but he made the name Lolly Pop two words instead of one.

George Smith was not only impressed with the horse, but also with its name. Perhaps he mused, "That would be a great name for my hard candy on a stick!" And so the Lolly Pop was born.

Courtesy Madeline Manella

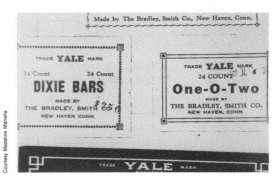
Courtesy Madeline Manella

Courtesy Madeline Manella

Bradley, Smith patented the name in 1931. The trademark couldn't be enforced, however, because the Bradley, Smith Company stopped making candy for awhile during the Depression in the mid-1930s. So the word became a generic one, spelled either lollypop or lollipop.

In the 1920s, when almost every confectioner got into the candy bar business, Bradley, Smith did too. The company produced a number of candy bars under the Yale trademark. (The well-known university was also in New Haven.)

All the Yale bar wrappers were white with navy blue borders and red print. (Blue and white were the colors of Yale University.) Many bars were made under the Yale trademark. The Graham Lunch bar consisted of two graham crackers with a layer of peanut buter dipped in milk chocolate. The B'Gosh bar had a marshmallow center surrounded by a layer of caramel that was dipped in dark chocolate. The Dixie bar was a peanut butter bar, and the M. M. Cocoanut bar had a center of white cream and coconut dipped in bitter chocolate. Other bars were Nut Mallow, Tingle Bar, Mallow Puff, Chocolate Covered Peanut Bar, and Chocolate Peanut Crunch.

The two bars with the biggest Yale connection were the Blue Boy bar and the Boo-La bar. The Blue Boy was named after a rather well-known Yale football player of the time, Albie Booth. His nickname was Little Boy Blue. The bar had a marshmallow center and was dipped in milk chocolate.

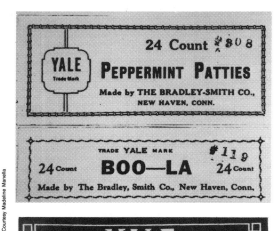

Although the Bradley, Smith Company wasn't aware of it, there actually was a football team nicknamed Blue Boys. Illinois College was founded in 1829 in Jacksonville, Illinois. A group of people from Yale known as the Yale Band was instrumental in starting the college. The school colors became blue and white, and the nickname for the college athletic teams became the Blue Boys. Had the folks in Illinois in later years known about the Blue Boy candy bar, it surely would have been a hit in Jacksonville.

In 1931, Bradley, Smith entered a combine with three other confectionery companies to manufacture and handle sales of the nationally advertised Believe It or Not! bar. Each of the companies in the combine had a specific sales territory. Bradley, Smith's was New England and New York City. The other companies were Minter Brothers of Philadelphia, Walter Johnson Candy Company of Chicago (with a factory in Los Angeles), and Imperial Candy Company of Seattle. Those three covered the rest of the country. The bar

sold well for only a few years before fading out during the Depression.

Bradley, Smith dropped the rest of its candy bar line during the mid-1930s, so the Yale trademark was put to rest. But while they were around, the blue-and-white-wrapper Yale bars developed quite a following.

Bradley, Smith Company, Inc., one hundred years old in 1983, is no longer in the lollypop or bar business, but is active as a distributor and packager of candy and other lines. Now in the hands of three capable women, the company, along with Yale, will continue to make sure New Haven stays on the map. After all, that's where Lolly Pops and Boo-La Boo-La got their start!

Living the Good Life

Three hundred years of German settlement in the United States was celebrated in 1983. The Germans have contributed many famous personalities in all walks of life—Albert Einstein, Marlene Dietrich, H. L. Mencken, and Babe Ruth, to name just a few.

One business in which many German immigrants made their mark was the confectionery business, and Otto J. Schoenleber of Milwaukee was no exception. First in the furniture business, he soon left it to enter the chocolate business with a newcomer who was a chocolate maker by trade.

The Ambrosia Chocolate Company opened May 9, 1894. The company name meant food of the gods and indicated that chocolate and cocoa were not only appetizing and delicious, but also of the finest quality. Schoenleber soon took over control of the company and by 1913 was joined in the business by his daughter Gretchen.

Early sales concentrated on consumer items such as penny goods and solid chocolate bars. Early favorites were Peter Peter Bars and Angel Food. Later, such bar items as Ambrosia Chocolate Bark,

Pecan Rounds, Milk Chocolate Cuts, Peanut Slabs, and Chocolate Nut-Chunk were added. And in the early 1930s, such bar items as Choc-lit Malted, Chocolate 'Sorted Nuts, Vanilla Chocolate, and Milk Chocolate were produced in the bun form that was becoming popular at the time.

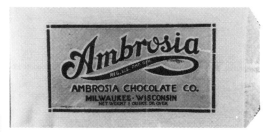

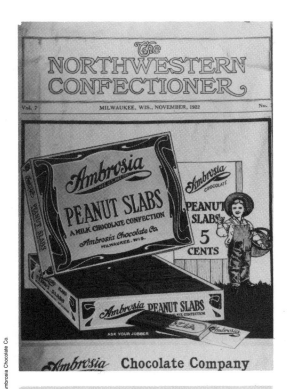

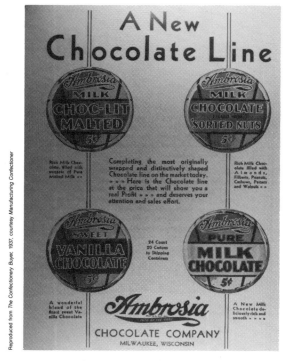

The Ambrosia Chocolate Company eventually got out of the bar business to concentrate on chocolate and cocoa products for the confectionery trade. In 1963, Ambrosia acquired the Hooten Chocolate Company, and in 1964 it merged with W. R. Grace and Company.

When Otto Schoenleber (his name roughly translates, "living the good life") started in the confectionery business about ninety years ago, he often advertised in German newspapers. One ad stated a philosophy that rings true for Ambrosia products to this day. "Bei allem besseren Händlern zu haben," means "available in all the better stores."

One Ambrosia product has been made for more than seventy-five years and is now available to the general public. It's called Tixies. Tixies are produced as twelve- and twenty-four-ounce sectioned bars on a limited basis only. Tixies are indeed scrumptious, but if you haven't been so fortunate as to taste one, you can at least savor Tixies vicariously through this description: "An extraordinary blend of satin-smooth Milk Chocolate enhanced with a Fondant Vanilla Chocolate for a hint of the continental flavor. This superb Chocolate is then carefully combined with mellow almonds, crisp pecans, and chewy cashews that have been tenderly toasted in pure cocoa butter." Like WOW!

Otto Schoenleber left a legacy of "living the good life" when he became involved in the confectionery business. May he munch contentedly on Tixies for eternity.

The Westward Ho Spirit

In 1843, the most prominent pathway to the West was the Oregon Trail. By 1846, it was well trodden.

In early May of each year, overland travelers gathered along the Missouri above the bend where the water turned sharply eastward at the mouth of the Kansas River. The prairies were then dry enough to carry heavy loads such as the settlers' covered wagons, called prairie schooners. These were similar to the heavy Conestoga or Pittsburgh wagons built by the Pennsylvania Dutch in the Susquehanna River region.

The prairie schooner had heavy wheels that carried a wide body. It was covered with a canvas top supported on bows of bent white oak. The wagons were drawn by horses or oxen, while some family members walked alongside driving cattle or other livestock. Groups of wagons created caravans along the Oregon Trail. The prairie schooner found its way over many other trails, too, to complete the settling of land beyond the Mississippi River.

To commemorate the significance of the prairie schooner in American history (and also to come up with a good name for a candy bar), Glade Candy Company of Salt Lake City came out with its first Prairie Schooner candy bar in 1928. The bar sold for five cents and had a different shape and formulation than the present-day Prairie Schooner bar, which is round, has a vanilla cream center, and is coated with chocolate studded with pecan pieces.

It was in 1916 that J. V. (Vern) Glade founded his candy business. He had thirty-five cents in his pocket when he decided to take the plunge in the kitchen of the Glade home in Salt Lake City. Glade had worked in his teens for Charles T. Prisk, who was in the confectionery and stationery business in Park City. It was while working for Prisk that Glade began to sense the potential in candy. At that time, the five-cent opera bar was being produced by numerous manufacturers.

In 1916, Glade finally turned to candy after working at other jobs. He became his own salesman and delivery boy. The first "big" order was for five dollars worth of peppermint chews to be delivered to a neighborhood grocer. The advance payment was used for supplies and as a down payment on a bicycle!

Within a few months, Glade had more than three hundred accounts for peppermint chews. A near tragedy almost closed down the one-man factory when Glade single-handedly tried pushing a seven hundred fifty-pound barrel of corn syrup up the back porch steps. The barrel got away and rolled down the steps, across the yard, and crashed through the back fence. Luckily, it didn't break, and production continued.

The Salt Lake City baseball team, which was in the Pacific Coast League at the time, created additional candy sales. Soon the growing business vacated the home kitchen to move to a new location.

The company was officially organized in 1922 and is now run by a second generation of Glades along with third-generation sons. The company's popular candy bars in the late 1920s and 1930s were Nut

Loaf, Opera Bar, Fruit Sandwich, Go Getter, Victoria Twins, and Cherry Twins.

Those bars were sold unwrapped in the 1920s, but were handwrapped in the 1930s. Other Glade bars of those times were Chocolate Pudding, Ruffit Fudge, Teddy Bar, Nutty Wonder, and Cherry Blossom. The Cherry Blossom bar is still being produced on a limited scale.

Today Glade's main production items are various forms and flavors of saltwater taffy and box chocolates (first made in the 1930s). But the Glade Prairie Schooner and Cherry Blossom are cheered by candy bar fans in the western part of the United States when they are found on candy counters.

The Laudatory Phrase Chocolate Bar

Betty Hutton, born Betty Jane Thornburg, was in her heyday as an American leading lady in many light entertainment singing and dancing movies in the 1940s. One of the many films she made was *The Perils of Pauline*, in 1947. And because of the success of that film, she was utilized in ads to help sell the Vita-Sert chocolate bar, manufactured by the Cook Chocolate Company of Chicago. The Cook Company not only used Hutton, but other movie

stars of the time, including Anne Jeffreys and Barbara Hale.

The Vita-Sert bar was one of the first bars to get into the vitamin kick that emerged in the 1940s. The wrapper listed the vitamins added to the bar as a sales gimmick. The bar, no longer around, was originated by Edmond Opler.

Opler started in the chocolate business in 1913 as a salesman for a New York chocolate manufacturer. He was sixteen at the time. After a stint in the Marines in World War I, Opler moved to Chicago, where he was involved in several cocoa ventures, and eventually became a partner in the chocolate-making Siren Mills in Chicago. The Nestlé Company soon bought Siren Mills but left the chocolate molds with Opler.

Those chocolate molds were the impetus for Opler to form the Cook Chocolate Company in the 1930s. One of the bars Opler began making in the 1940s was named World's Finest. When he tried to register the name as a trademark, he couldn't get approval from Washington. He was told that the two words were just a laudatory phrase, and couldn't be registered. Mr. Opler then asked, "Well, what about the Pure in Pure Oil Company?" The response was that Pure was part of a company name. Opler eventually decided to change his company's name from Cook Chocolate Company to World's Finest Chocolate, Inc., in the late 1940s.

The Cook name is used for a few products today, but it is as World's Finest that the company produces chocolate bars by the score for fundraising groups around the country. Bars are also made for private clubs, hotels, and restaurants, and to special order. For example, bars for baby gifts are made to match the newborn's weight. Opler's biggest bar was a two hundred twenty-five pound chocolate that McDonald's of New York presented to the Ronald McDonald Houses in 1983.

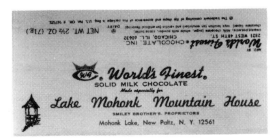

Opler got into the fund-raising business by accident. One of his salesmen was calling on a drugstore in Zion, Illinois, in the 1940s. The druggist was strongly supportive of school athletics, and he asked the salesman if some chocolate bars could be provided to raise money. Opler accommodated the druggist's request, and World's Finest geared up its production line to turn out its ingot-shaped bars in personalized white wrappers.

The bar certainly has established itself as a much-enjoyed candy treat throughout the United States, thanks to the far-sightedness of Edmond Opler, Sr., who was still going strong at age eighty-eight in 1985!

Mother's Name Was Emily

It all started in a kitchen in 1933 in Altoona, Pennsylvania. That's when Bill Boyer turned out his first batch of whipped cream fudge. His brother Bob took over from there by canvassing Altoona, making sales from a basket hung over his arm.

It wasn't long before Mrs. Emily Boyer, mother of the boys, took a hand. She began to supervise the fudge-making department by moving it to the basement, where the boys made their products by hand. Chocolate items were added and, when warm weather approached, work had to be done on cool nights. In those days, adequate refrigeration for setting chocolate wasn't available.

Eventually, the Boyers needed more space, so they moved to larger quarters in a frame building next to the Boyer home. In 1939, the plant was moved to its present location in Altoona.

In 1939, the Boyer Brothers Candy Company came into its own with the Mallo Cup. Until that time, fudge, small candies, and Easter eggs were Boyer's products. But Mallo Cup, containing chocolate and ground coconut surrounding a center of marshmallow cream, was offered that year to the jobbing trade in western Pennsylvania. In the 1940s, an Almond Mallo bar was manufactured. Cup-O-Cocoanut and Jamboree were also produced.

In 1955, Boyer Brothers was one of the first companies to receive liquid chocolate in tank trucks. Corn syrup and liquid sugar were also supplied in the same way.

Along with its candy lines, the company served the ice cream trade with bulk products such as marshmallow, chocolate, butterscotch, and natural caramel flavors. Later Bill Boyer developed a natural peanut butter for ice cream manufacturers that could be used in and over solid or soft ice cream. This product has become a staple for large and small ice cream manufacturers throughout the United States.

In 1969, Boyer Brothers was sold to American Maize Products Company. The Boyer brothers remained associated in various roles until the mid-1970s. Consoli-

dated Brands of Ridgewood, New York, took over in mid-1984.

In 1969, the four leading items in the line of cup candies were Mallo Cup, Smoothie, Peanut Butter Cup, and Mint Mallo.

The Boyers, Bill and Bob, became successes in business. And they were certainly representative of the old adage, "Behind every successful boy stands his mother." In the Boyer's case, her name was Emily.

Buffalo Bill and Frank's Buffalo

William Frederick Cody was a frontiersman who later became an entertainer. Soon after the Civil War, he took a job as a hunter for a company that was supplying meat to the construction crews on the Kansas Pacific Railroad. Cody killed several thousand buffalo while on the job. Because of his involvement with that mammal, he later was dubbed Buffalo Bill by the writer Z. C. Judson.

Judson, writing under the pen name Ned Buntline, met Cody in 1869. As Buntline, he began to feature Buffalo Bill in a series of fictional adventures that appeared as dime novels. The little paperback volumes soon made Cody a well-known figure throughout the world.

Frank Hoyt also dealt with the buffalo, but under somewhat different circumstances. In 1901, Hoyt started his own business as a confectioner and purveyor of the peanut in various forms. Frank, undoubtedly an avid reader of the Buffalo Bill dime novels in his youth, thought the buffalo would be a noble animal to serve as the symbol for his products. And so was born the Buffalo Brand trademark for Hoyt's company, F. M. Hoyt and Company, Inc., in Amesbury, Massachusetts.

In his early years as a businessman, Hoyt came across a massive, mounted buffalo head. His eyes lit up when he saw it, and he immediately purchased it to hang on the wall behind his office desk. Over the years in that office, as Frank worked at his bookkeeping, the buffalo head peered over his shoulder. Visitors found it to be quite a conversation piece.

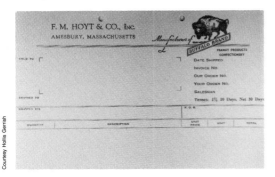

Courtesy Hollis Gerrish

Frank Hoyt ran the company until the late 1940s, when he turned over control to George Batchelder. Even though the company changed hands, the buffalo head remained on the office wall. In the late 1950s, the Squirrel Brand Company of Cambridge, Massachusetts, bought out the Hoyt company. Company records and products were taken over and moved to Cambridge, but various office items were disposed of at auction. The buffalo head was one of those items.

By now, Hoyt's buffalo head had become an institution in the area of Massachusetts bordering New Hampshire, so the buffalo head was the highlight of the auction. After spirited bidding, Bossy Gillis, mayor of the neighboring town of Newburyport, won the prize. Gillis proudly installed the buffalo head on the wall of his gas station in Newburyport, where it then gazed out the window glass at the gas pumps. Over the years, that buffalo head became part of the scenery, but it eventually disappeared. Unfortunately, its whereabouts are now unknown.

While active in the company, Frank Hoyt was persistent in tracking down delinquent accounts. One such account had been established in 1938 and finally was taken to court in 1942. Through voluminous correspondence and various court orders, Hoyt finally collected the sum of $27.99 to close out the account.

The best-known Hoyt products over the years were associated with the peanut and peanut butter. Hoyt's Buffalo Brand Ruff-Cut Peanut Butter was the first peanut butter on the market containing pieces of whole peanuts. Along with regular peanut butter, it was a Hoyt staple for many years.

Candy with peanut butter centers were also popular Hoyt products. Hoyt But-A-Kiss candies were leaders in that line. Also made by Hoyt was saltwater taffy. It was packaged under numerous trade names other than Buffalo Brand. Jane Winslow and Brook Farm Candies are two examples.

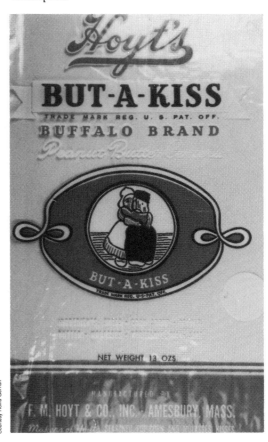

Courtesy Hollis Gerrish

Three of Hoyt's 1930s products were fourteen-ounce candy bars. They were Hoyt's Chocolate Nutty Fruit bar, Chocolate Nut Bar, and Chocolate Buffalo Barque. Hoyt drew up his own ideas of what the wrappers should look like. The wrapper-making company's art department, using Hoyt's rough sketches as models, executed the final designs.

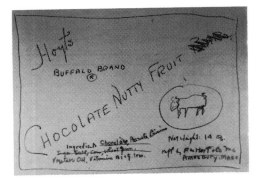

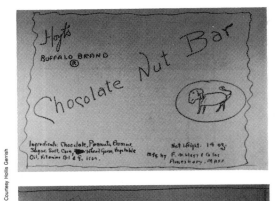

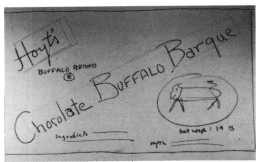

Several Hoyt candy bars were also produced in the 1940s, and they all featured peanuts in one form or another. Two of the better selling bars were Peanut Krunch Bar and Peanut Butter Betty. Appealing to the World War II crowd were Just-A-Kiss molasses kisses. The package wrapper showed a sailor popping one of the candy kisses into the mouth of a comely lass on a pier.

The Buffalo Brand trademark disappeared from some of the later products but was never really replaced as a symbol for

Hoyt's company. The company is long gone, but its labels can still be seen on peanut butter containers that are prized possessions of antique advertising collectors. Of course, the labels feature a picture of the animal that held such a fascination for Hoyt—the buffalo.

46

It Pays to Be Observant

The young salesman was making his rounds to Mom and Pop grocery stores prior to America's entry into World War I. In store after store, he saw a scene repeated. A clerk would dip his or her often grimy hands into open candy jars, take out some candy, drop it on a scale, and make a sale of around one or two cents.

The young salesman, Walter Reid, Jr., particularly noticed three things: the clerk was often overly generous in weighing the candy; seldom was the sale for as much as a nickel; and fruit tablets were one of the most popular items sold.

A bell rang in the mind of this young entrepreneur. Why not create a fruit tablet that would achieve three goals? It would eliminate unsanitary handling of the candy pieces; do away with profit losses resulting from careless weighing, and encourage larger unit sales.

Reid's family and friends agreed, and soon money was gathered to start the Charms Company to make Charms fruit tablets in a small loft in Newark, New Jersey.

When America entered the war in 1917, Reid convinced the War Department that his Lemon Charms would make a convenient, tasty, and wholesome addition to field rations. Soon Lemon Charms were being shipped to U. S. forces overseas.

As a result of the war effort, Lemon Charms became one of the most popular items on the nation's candy counters. By 1919, there were ten additional flavors. Eventually Charms pioneered a machine that wrapped each fruit table individually and then collectively in a colorful foil outer wrapper.

The rapidly growing Charms Company obtained a larger factory in Bloomfield, New Jersey. It was here that a line of candy bars (now discontinued) was developed in the late 1930s and sold into the early 1940s. Some of those candy bar items were Rum & Raisin, Pecan Brittle,

Peanut Brittle Charms, Charms Cocoanut, Charms Jellies, Gold Standard, and Chevron.

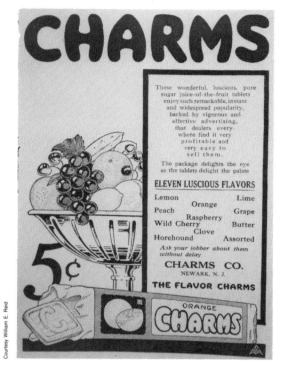

Courtesy William E. Reid

Courtesy William E. Reid

Courtesy William E. Reid

47

Charms lollipops became a big seller in the 1960s. Another item, Charms Blow Pops (a bubble-gum-filled center in a hard-candy jacket) came along soon thereafter.

Now located in Colts Neck, New Jersey, the Charms Company continues the business that Walter Reid, Jr. started by being observant.

Fanne, Fannie, and Fanny

Remember Fanne Foxe? She's the stripper Wilbur Mills pursued along the Tidal Basin in Washington, D.C., in 1974.

Now what about Fannie Merrit Farmer? She was a Boston woman of merit. Born in 1857, she suffered a paralytic stroke while in high school that abruptly ended her formal education. She recovered from the paralysis enough to help around the house, and she developed a fondness for cooking. Despite her handicap, she refused to become a recluse and instead embarked on a career in cookery that was to establish her as one of the leaders in the field. She graduated from the Boston Cooking School and eventually became its leader. But she left to form Miss Farmer's School of Cookery in 1902. At her school, courses were designed to train housewives rather than servants. For one year, she also taught a course in invalid cooking at Harvard.

She and a sister wrote a regular column for the popular magazine *Woman's Home Companion*. The column ran for ten years. One of Fannie Farmer's many accomplishments was the introduction to cooking of standard measurements, such as the level teaspoon and level cup. She also published several cookbooks. *The Boston Cooking School Cookbook* was first published in 1896 is still a best seller in a frequently revised modernized version, *The Fannie Farmer Cookbook*.

Several years before her death, Fannie suffered another stroke, but this didn't deter her from her appointed rounds. She continued to lecture from a wheelchair. In fact, her last lecture preceded her death in 1915 by only ten days.

A truly remarkable woman, her career fascinated a gentleman ·named Frank O'Connor. He opened the first of many candy shops in 1919 in Rochester, New York. In recognition of the famous Fannie Farmer, he decided to name his candy shops in her honor, but he changed the spelling of Fannie to Fanny. Today Fanny Farmer candies are sold in about three hundred thirty shops in twenty-two states and in more than six hundred department stores, as well as military installations from coast to coast. Fanny Farmer headquarters are located in Bedford, Massachussetts.

Fanny Farmer makes candy bars such as Chocolate Marshmallow Caramel, Milk Chocolate, French Chocolate, Chocolate French Mint, Frosted French Mint, Mint Pattie, and Peanut Butter bars. Fanny Farmer Candy Shops, Inc., now owns all rights to the Fannie Farmer name, including the world-famous cookbook.

Now that we've had a chance to discuss both Fannie and Fanny, we can get back to Fanne for a moment. She, as far as we know, remains a free spirit. But if you were to pause for a few seconds along the Tidal Basin in Washington, D.C., on a still night, you just might hear the ghostly footsteps echoing from that first (and last) running of the Wilbur Mills Futurity.

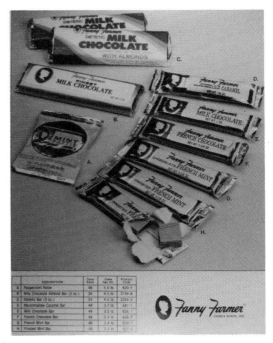

The Big Rock

Early in the nineteenth century, a family named Spencer set sail from England to the New World. Disaster overtook them, and the family lost all its worldly goods in a shipwreck. By the time the Spencers reached Salem, Massachusetts, in 1806, they were in sad shape.

Salem neighbors, aware of the family's destitute straits, pitched in to help. Knowing that Mrs. Spencer was a candy maker, they donated a barrel of sugar. From that barrel Mrs. Spencer produced candy that was sold from a pail on the steps of a Salem church. That candy was to make her famous as the lady who created Gibralters.

Gibralters quickly became a sought-after treat, and storekeepers put placards in their windows saying that the candy was available inside.

Her business established, Mrs. Spencer soon had enough money to buy a horse and wagon, from which she peddled her wares. After her death, her son continued the business until it was taken over by a Mr. Pepper. The company, now run by the Burkinshaw family and called Ye Olde

49

Pepper Companie is located across the parking area from the historic House of Seven Gables in Salem.

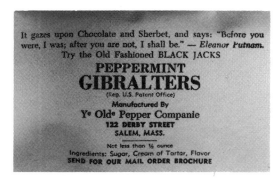

It gazes upon Chocolate and Sherbet, and says: "Before you were, I was; after you are not, I shall be." — *Eleanor Putnam.*

Try the Old Fashioned BLACK JACKS

PEPPERMINT

GIBRALTERS

(Reg. U.S. Patent Office)

Manufactured By

Ye Olde Pepper Companie

122 DERBY STREET
SALEM, MASS.

Not less than ⅛ ounce

Ingredients: Sugar, Cream of Tartar, Flavor

SEND FOR OUR MAIL ORDER BROCHURE

The Gibralter, considered the first commercially sold and continuously made candy in America, is a diamond-shaped bar of peppermint or lemon-flavored hard candy that ages gracefully. A jar of Gibralters more than one-hundred-fifty years old resides in a container in the present Ye Olde Pepper Companie store. For years the Burkinshaws sampled a Gibralter from the jar each Christmas and declared it as tasty as freshly made ones. The annual Christmas tasting was given up a few years ago, however, because the supply of antique Gibralters was running low. The jar stands on a shelf in the store for all to admire.

Where did the name Gibralter come from? During that fateful voyage from England to the New World, the ship carrying the Spencer family passed near the Straits of Gibraltar. Mrs. Spencer was most impressed by the big rock guarding one side of the straits. Later, when she began to make the candy from the recipe she had gotten from a sailor, the name Gibraltar came to mind.

As luck would have it, the printer who was commissioned to print labels for the candy wasn't the world's best speller. He substituted an "e" for the final "a" in Gibraltar and came up with Gibralter. Suffice it to say, the spelling stuck.

Because they kept so well, Gibralters sailed with Salem whalers. More recently they were chronicled in a book by Elizabeth Coatsworth, *Runaway Home*, a history and travel book for children. Two pages of the book were devoted to Salem Gibralters.

Attesting to the longevity of this famous candy, the wrapper carries Eleanor Putnam's romantic riddle, "Before you were, I was; after you are not, I shall be." Roughly translated, this means "Gibralters forever."

Tales of Hoffman

E. T. A. Hoffmann was a famous German composer and author in the early 1800s. Another composer, Jacques Offenbach, immortalized Hoffmann in his operetta, "Tales of Hoffmann."

About one hundred years later, another Hoffman came along—this time spelled with only one "n." His bailiwick was Los Angeles, California. E. A. Hoffman started making candies on his stove at night after work. That was the beginning of the Hoffman Candy Company of Los Angeles, which has served Southern California and the West for more than seventy years.

In the early 1920s, Hoffman was joined in his business by Ben Myerson. The two men crafted fine candy bars, some of which are still enjoyed today. (Myerson later left to form his own company.) The Cherry A-Let bar was introduced in the early 1920s. And the first candy cup product manufactured in America, according to company records, was the Choc

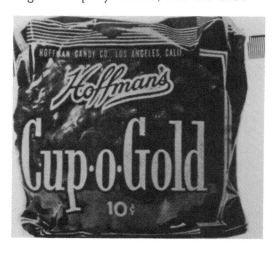

Shop bar, introduced in the early 1930s. It was followed in 1935 by the bar that established Hoffman's reputation—the Cup-o-Gold bar. Those three bars are still produced, as are such bars as Chocolate Mint and Peanut Cluster.

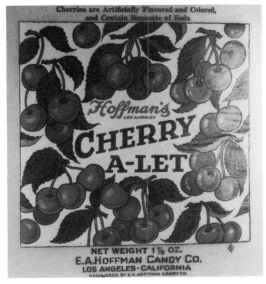

In the 1930s, Hoffman candy racks and wooden display boxes featured an assortment of Hoffman bars at the price of three for ten cents. Such bars as Milk-A-Let, Inside Stuff, Coco-A-Let, Butter Toffee, Wizard, Almond-A-Let, Chocolate Wafers, and The Habit were offered along with many of the previously mentioned bars. Other early Hoffman bars were Chicken Bone, Nut and Date, and Butter-Smack.

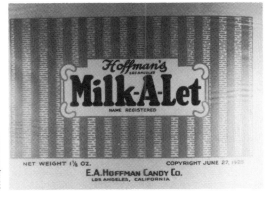

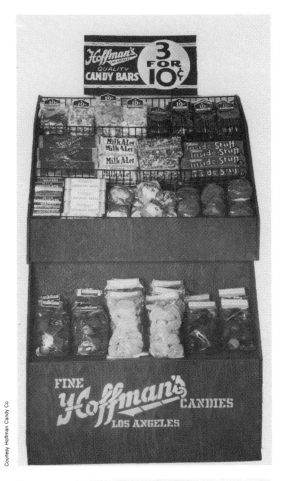

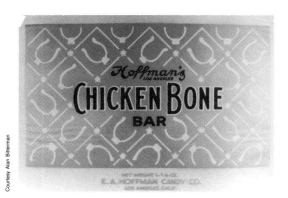

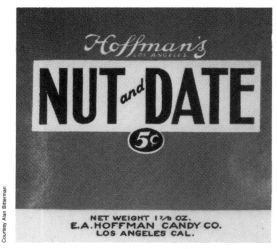

Roadside America

It was in 1925 that a young man took over the operation of a small patent medicine store with a soda fountain and a newsstand located in a small section of Quincy, Massachusetts, known as Wollaston. The young man quickly turned a money-losing operation into a successful business.

At the soda fountain three commercial flavors of ice cream were sold—vanilla, chocolate, and strawberry. The young man thought a wider variety of flavors and a better quality of ice cream would be the keys to success. He used an old-fashioned freezer in the basement and, experimenting with recipes, began cranking the handle of the freezer to produce the ice cream that was to make Howard Deering Johnson's fortune.

Soon customers were standing in line outside his small store to buy his ice cream. Shortly he was selling it at small stands on nearby beaches and other locations.

To his successful ice cream business he added frankfurters, hamburgers, and other foods that could be easily prepared. His little confectionery store had evolved into a restaurant, and Johnson decided the food business was the way to go.

In 1929, he opened another restaurant and then entered the franchising business. The familiar Howard Johnson's bright orange roof quickly became a landmark along the Atlantic coast and later along highway and tollways throughout the country. Motor lodges were soon to follow.

Johnson pioneered the now common "convenience food" concept of proportioning food and processing it in central company-operated plants from which it was shipped to restaurants for final preparation and cooking.

In the 1940s, a Coconut candy bar was made for the company by another organization, but the wrapper had the Howard Johnson's label on it. By 1957, bars

Touch Down and Trojan Twins were two Hoffman candy bars with football connections. Trojans was the nickname for the University of Southern California's team, and twin bars were packed in a Trojan Twins package. The Touch Down bar indicated to a customer that he or she was scoring by buying that Hoffman product.

The two football-related candy bars are no longer around, but other Hoffman bars continue to keep folks in Southern California and the West happy with sweet thoughts.

began to be made in company-owned factories. Subsequently other bars such as Fudge Bar, Fiesta Bar, Crispette Bar, Caramel Peanut Bar, and Peppermint Bar appeared for distribution to Howard Johnson's restaurants.

Howard Deering Johnson was indeed a man with a vision. One wonders what might have happened to the candy bar business had he decided to go into it rather than ice cream. No doubt he'd have been worthy competition for others in the trade. Would his first bar have been named the HJ Bar and sold in an orange wrapper?

Head for the Mountains— Owyhee, That Is

In 1778, Captain James Cook discovered some beautiful islands in the Pacific. The natives called their land Hawaii, but that name didn't suit Captain Cook. He marked the islands on his map as the Sandwich Islands. He wanted to honor the Earl of Sandwich, who, legend tells us, was the first to eat meat between two pieces of bread. For many years, maps showed the Sandwich Islands, but eventually the native name of Hawaii began to appear.

In 1819, three Polynesian miners (or fur trappers, according to another report) set out on an expedition to southwestern Idaho. They disappeared and were never heard from again. When local residents of Idaho were asked where the lost trio was from, one of the locals said, "Owyhee." That's the best he could do to reproduce what the Polynesians called their homeland, Hawaii.

The peculiar spelling (and pronunciation) of Hawaii still is used in Idaho. There's a river, a mountain range, a county, and a museum named Owyhee in memory of the three lost explorers. There's also a candy company that commemorates that name on its candy bar wrappers.

Idaho is known as the potato state, and Idaho potatoes, or spuds, are the aristocrats of the potato world. In 1927, two big firsts took place. Charles Lindbergh made his solo flight across the Atlantic, and T. O. Smith came up with

the first candy bar named after a vegetable, Idaho Spud.

The Idaho Candy Company was founded in 1901 in Boise. The founder, T. O. Smith, created the Idaho Spud bar which carried the motto, "Owyhee Idaho Spud—the candy bar that makes Idaho famous." Other candy companies came out with similarly named bars. Dainty Maid of Pocatello, Idaho, had an Idaho Russet bar, and Ostler Candy Company of Salt Lake City had a Spud Bar. Those two bars are no longer around.

The Idaho Spud originally was made of two halves. Each half looked like a chocolate- and coconut-covered potato. When automation came into its own, a single bar was packaged in the wrapper. The center of the bar remained a chocolate-flavored marshmallow.

The bar's colorful potato-brown wrapper is covered with two dozen potato eyes, wearing horn-rimmed glasses. The artist who drew the eyes got a bit carried away, so the eyes have more of a lemony than a spud look.

While the Idaho Spud is the company's most famous bar, other candy bars have been on the production line. Two bars produced from the 1930s to the early 1970s were the Quarter Section and Big Eats bars. A Mint Pattie and a Cherry Cocktail bar, as well as an Idaho Toasted Taters bar, were also made for awhile.

54

Still around to keep the Idaho Spud Company rolling is the Old Faithful bar, a nut roll named after Yellowstone Park's most famous geyser. At Christmas time, many Idahoans send boxes of Idaho Spud candy bars to friends and relatives throughout the world. The boxes are shipped to spread the word that spuds, as well as Owyhee, have indeed put Idaho on the map.

On, Wisconsin!

Who had the first and second largest incomes in the state of Wisconsin in 1920? Two fellows in the candy business, William Kuhn and William Stark, the largest stockholders in the American Candy Company of Milwaukee, Wisconsin. Back in those days, there were no capital gains.

The American Candy Company was founded in 1888 by William Stark, who had previously worked for Ziegler Candy Company as a bookkeeper. At Ziegler, Stark produced an ornamental bookkeeping script that was embellished with a flourish known in German as a *Schnorkel*. His boss, George Ziegler, often good-naturedly complained, "Cut it out mit all those Schnorkels, my lad."

The word Schnorkels, so the story goes, stuck with Stark, and eventually evolved into the candy bar name Snirkles, first produced in the 1920s by American Candy.

American Candy was liquidated in 1938. But during the company's heyday, numerous candy bars were manufactured. Wise Cracks and Peanut Turtle (more about this bar later) were good sellers in the late 1920s and early 1930s. Some of the American Candy Company bars, in addition to the bar name, carried the identification label "Rex" and a logo of a crown. Some of the Rex-identified bars were Who's Who, Longfellow, Malted Milk, and Wafers.

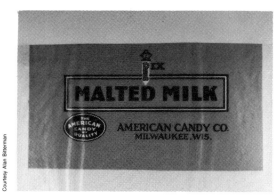

Upon liquidation of American Candy, Howard B. Stark, William's son, bought some of the equipment and started his own company, the Howard B. Stark Company. Numerous candy items were developed, and the Snirkles bar was continued. In the late 1950s, licorice and chocolate

versions of Snirkles were also on the market.

The main plant is located in Pewaukee, Wisconsin, and a second factory is in Thibodaux, Louisiana. William F. Stark, now president of the company, wears two hats—one as a candy man exemplar, and the second as an author. Among his works is an excellent historical volume, *Ghost Towns of Wisconsin*, published in 1977.

The last of the Wisconsin ghost towns mentioned in the book was Turtleville, established on Turtle Creek in 1838. By 1850, it was a bustling community, but declined during the early decades of this century and then faded away to a ghost town. It is likely that the American Candy Company's Peanut Turtle candy bar was named after Turtle Creek.

Turtleville, American Candy Company, and Peanut Turtle candy bars are just Wisconsin memories now. But still real is the Howard B. Stark Company, which turns out candy products to keep Wisconsin on the confectionery map of the United States.

How Sweet It Is

In 1890, Leon Sweet began a sweet business in Portland, Oregon. Sweet decided to move to Salt Lake City in 1900, and the Sweet Candy Company soon became a fixture in the city beside the inland saltwater lake.

Making a general line of candy, Sweet began candy bar production after World War I ended. Sweet candy bars were soon popular in Salt Lake City in such places as the old Salt Palace, where bicycle races were held, and in Salt Lake City theaters. Boys with trays strolled through the audience selling such favorites as Sweet's Opera Bar and Nut Loaf Bars. Along with the five cent bars, ten cent bars were produced.

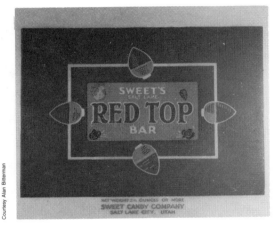

Other old-time Sweet bars were Rough Rider, Alabama Hot Cakes, Red Top, Frosted Cocoanut, and Hollywood Stars. Polar Bar was another old-time bar whose wrapper pictured a polar bear. The play on words had two meanings—bar as in candy bar, and bar as in bear, the way Davy Crockett pronounced it. All these bars sold respectably in the late 1920s and 1930s.

Sweet discontinued its candy bars in the early 1970s and now produces a general line of candy, plus saltwater taffy and tasty chocolate-covered orange sticks.

Chuckwagon was the last candy bar off the Sweet production line. All in all, Sweet made about sixty different candy bars over the years. While they were around, no doubt they managed to sweeten the lives of all who came in contact with them.

Sock It to 'Em, Preacher

It was 1872, and things in Portland, Maine, were jumping. Everyone in town was talking about the goings-on at the town's meeting hall, where the Reverend George S. Needham of Needham, Massachusetts, was holding a series of evangelical meetings. The meetings were most popular, and Needham's name was on everyone's tongue.

A gentleman named Allen Gow ran a confectionery store in Portland. One Monday morning, the day after Reverend Needham had conducted a most inspirational session, Gow arrived at his store to find his candy makers producing square, bar-shaped batches of creamy coconut fondant dipped into bittersweet chocolate. "What are you going to call the new candy?" Gow asked one of the candy makers.

Mr. Ellsworth, the candy maker, smiled. He had heard the electrifying Reverend Needham the previous evening, so he said with authority, "Call them Needhams!"

After Ellsworth made the first Needhams, bars made by others using the Needham name were made. In the late 1920s and 1930s, for example, the Spear Folks Company of Portland made a Needham, as did the Maine Confectionery Company of Saco, Maine. Its bar was called Maine Made Need-Em.

Another long-time maker of the bar was the Seavey Company, which made Seavey's Needham. That company was purchased by Lou-Rod Candy, Inc., of Lewiston, Maine, in 1960. For a while, Lou-Rod made their own Lou Rod Needham and a Sugarloaf Needham, but the company discontinued them to concentrate on the Seavey's Needham, packaged in an open-ended bag of bright orange, blue, and white. Preacher Needham would certainly be mighty proud of his continuing candy namesake.

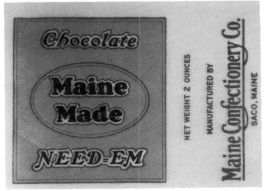

The Big Train

Voted the American League's most valuable player in 1924, Walter P. Johnson was one of baseball's premier pitchers. He toiled for twenty-one years for the Washington Senators and, due to his superlative pitching skills, earned the nickname "Big Train." His fast ball was considered one of the fastest of all time.

Another Walter Johnson (with an H as the middle initial) could have been considered one of the "Big Trains" of the early candy bar business. It was 1925 when Walter H. Johnson, shortly after the introduction of the Bit-O-Honey bar, broke away from the Schutter-Johnson Candy Company to form his own company, the Walter H. Johnson Candy Company in Chicago.

To acquaint the public with his Power-House candy bar, cartoon characters were painted on retail store windows. The campaign proved to be effective for a number of years. By the mid- to late 1940s (after the purchase of the Bishop and Company, Inc., confectionery in Los Angeles in 1944), the cartoon campaign moved to the Sunday comic pages nationwide. Roger Wilco became one of the comic character spokespersons for PowerHouse. Now made by Peter Paul Cadbury, Power-House is the only bar remaining from the many that Johnson produced over the years.

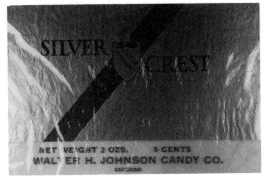

KINDLY NOTE:
Long John
IS DIFFERENT
LOOK!

CREAMY
CHEWY CENTER—
COVERED WITH
REAL MILK
CHOCOLATE

Long John
5¢

Soft, Creamy, Chewy Candy~
WALTER H. JOHNSON CANDY CO. Chicago, Ill.

It's **Spiffy**

NET WEIGHT 1¼ OZ.
WALTER H. JOHNSON CANDY COMPANY
CHICAGO, U.S.A.

WALTER JOHNSON'S
Long John
CREAMY, CHEWY CENTER

WALTER JOHNSON'S
Creamy Whipt
5¢

NET WEIGHT 1¾ OZ OR OVER.
WALTER H. JOHNSON CANDY CO.
CHICAGO, U.S.A.

WALTER JOHNSON'S
ROLL-ETTE

NET WEIGHT 1¾ OZ.
WALTER JOHNSON CANDY CO.
CHICAGO

NET WEIGHT 3 OZ.
5¢
WALTER JOHNSON'S
NUGAT CHEWS
PROOF *of the* PUDDING CANDIES
"IT'S IN THE EATING"

WALTER H. JOHNSON CANDY CO.
CHICAGO. ILL.

Tasty Time
**MALTED
MILK BAR**

NET WEIGHT 1 OZ. OR OVER.
WALTER H. JOHNSON CANDY CO.
CHICAGO

Weber's
ORIGINAL
ISABAR
TRADE MARK   REGISTERED

NET WEIGHT 1¼ OZ.
MANUFACTURED BY
WALTER H. JOHNSON CANDY CO.
CHICAGO, ILL.

Some of the many Johnson candies were Silver Crest, Long John, Roll-Ette, and Tasty Time. Others were Malted Milk Bar, Toasted Mels, It's Spiffy, Pecan Mel, Creamy Whipt, Nugat Chews, and Weber's Original Isabar.

Several Johnson items contained two bars in the wrapper and sold for five cents. Shirly Ann, Almond Delight, Milk Nougat, and Malted Milk Bar were examples. A popular late-1950s bar was Buttersweet Fudge, which sold for ten cents.

Johnson also made numerous bars that were utilized as prizes on the punchboards popular at the time. Two of them were Dash-O-Almonds and Brown Beauty, labeled as one-, two-, or three-cent bars. A third was the Crow OK bar. Sorry to say, none of those bars are still around, but then neither are the two Big Trains or Roger Wilco. Over and out:

Name Dropping

In the 1920s, confectioners often latched onto an immediately recognizable name for a candy bar. Two such names were Betsy Ross and Charles Lindbergh.

Betsy Ross (1752–1836) suggested a flag design to George Washington when America was preparing to declare its independence. She then made the famous flag in her back parlor from a sketch Washington made and thus found her place in history as an American patriot.

To capitalize on the popularity of her name some hundred years later, the W. E. Jacobs Candy Company of Chicago came out with The Betsy Ross Bar (subtitled "Loved by the Nation") in the mid-1920s. The bar was later made briefly by Walter H. Johnson Candy Company.

When Charles Lindbergh made his lonely flight across the Atlantic in 1927, he carried five sandwiches (but no candy bars) aboard the Spirit of St. Louis. Little did Lindbergh know that toward the end of the 1920s, the A. G. Morse Company of Chicago would zero in on his historic achievement by manufacturing the Winning Lindy candy bar. The Winning Lindy bar didn't last long in the marketplace. But at least Charles Lindbergh had a bar named after him—an honor Douglas Corrigan never received. Remember Douglas Corrigan? He was the American aviator who left New York for Los Angeles in 1939 and landed in Ireland, earning the nickname, "Wrong Way Corrigan." Who in the heck would ever come out with a Wrong Way Candy Bar?

Courtesy Glenn Sontag

Moonlight Serenade

When it comes to nuts, the Fisher Nut Company of St. Paul, Minnesota, has been around for quite a few years. But when it was known as the Fisher Nut and Chocolate Company, it wasn't in the candy bar business for long. It was in the early 1940s when their candy bar production started, and in the mid-1940s, production stopped. Getting out of the bar business

was perhaps due to competition in the marketplace and the difficulty of obtaining sugar during wartime rationing.

Two of the bars Fisher produced, with the delightful names of Daylight and Moonlight, were around for only about eight months. Where did the names come from? No one knows for sure, but perhaps the Daylight bar was turned out by the regular shift, and the Moonlight bar by the night shift.

Other Fisher bars included Cherry Hit, which had a wrapper picturing bunches of cherries. The bar was one of many on the market at the time that featured cherries in one form or another. The Kingfisher, another Fisher candy product, was a coconut-peanut bar.

Fisher did utilize its expertise in the nut business by producing Salted Nut Roll, which sold for five cents. Of all its bars, this was perhaps the best seller. It, too, faded away when Fisher dropped bar production completely in the mid-1940s to devote itself to nuts.

A mystery bar, Pine Apps, bears the name "Fisher's" on the wrapper, which dates to the late 1920s. It could very well have been a quickie Fisher product that was only on the market for a short time. Containing no nuts, the bar consisted of pineapple chunks covered with milk chocolate.

Courtesy Audrey and John Glenn

Elmer's Tune

One of the hit songs near the end of 1941 was "Elmer's Tune." The song was based on a bit of a melody whistled by Elmer Albrecht, one of the tune's three composers. One of the other composers was Dick Jurgens, a popular bandleader, who was one of the regulars at Chicago's Aragon and Trianon Ballrooms, popular dance emporiums of the times.

Many years earlier, in 1914, another Elmer's tune was played in New Orleans when the Elmer Candy Company was officially launched. The company had been known as the Miller-Elmer Candy Company and the Miller Candy Company before that.

Christopher Miller was sixteen when he walked down a gangplank to the New Orleans levee. It was 1845, and Miller, an immigrant from Germany, was seeking his fortune. The youngster found his first job as an assistant in a pastry shop. After three years, he grew restless and got the urge to travel, so he went to Cincinnati for six months, before returning to his job in New Orleans. Soon Miller advanced to the confectionery department in the shop, and that's when dreams of having his own business began.

Miller again left New Orleans, stopping in St. Louis in 1849 and journeying west to California in 1850. It was in San Francisco that Miller, along with a partner, opened a pastry shop that quickly became a favorite of the goldminers. Because of its popularity, the shop was soon moved from one mining area to another. Miller, it seems, struck it as rich as the miners who found a gold vein in the mountains.

Miller and his partner eventually had a parting of the ways, and Miller continued the business. But before long he again got homesick for New Orleans. He took passage from San Francisco aboard a ship that became shipwrecked off Santa Barbara. All passengers were saved, and Miller continued on his trip, eventually to arrive in Balboa, Panama. He crossed the isthmus by mule and riverboat and boarded a ship bound for New Orleans at Colon. Miller finally reached his favorite city in 1854.

In 1855, Miller's dreams were realized when the doors of the Miller Candy Company were opened. Over the years it had several locations in the city. Christopher Miller died in 1902, but the business was carried on by family members. One of the thirteen Miller children, a daughter named Olivia, had married Augustus Elmer, who became a favorite son-in-law of Miller. Soon after the turn of the century, Elmer and three of his brothers-in-law were admitted to the firm. At that time, the company became Miller-Elmer, and in later years it was known as the Elmer Candy Company.

New Orleans was and still is famous for its pecan pralines, but the city has another favorite candy creation—Heavenly Hash, a combination of milk chocolate, marshmallow, and toasted pecans. Heavenly Hash became a Southern favorite around the turn of the century. It was produced in a tiny confectionery shop in New Orleans, where it was sold in bulk for almost two decades. In 1923, Elmer's bought the recipe and the copyrighted name, then manufactured it and packaged it in various sized boxes. A candy bar version was also produced for a number of years.

Courtesy Alan Bitterman

In the 1920s and 1930s, Elmer's made a number of candy bars. Elmer's Best Bar was a chocolate malted milk confection. Jolly Boy was a milk chocolate nut roll. A companion to that bar was the Jolly Papa bar. Other bars of those times were Angel's Delight and Quality Bar.

Elmer's most famous bar, Gold Brick, was first manufactured in 1936. The name was probably chosen because of Christopher Miller's association with the Gold Rush Days. Gold Brick was introduced as a one-ounce candy bar that sold for five cents. At that time, numerous five cent candy bars weighed around four ounces, so the critics didn't expect

Gold Brick to last. But this chocolate bar, filled with pecans and double-coated with milk chocolate, fooled the critics. The bar found friends throughout the United States and is still a favorite today.

Gold Brick is the only candy bar now produced and sold year-round by Elmer's, which is now located in Ponchatoula, Louisiana. But other items such as fancy boxed chocolates and nuts, are also sold. Seasonal items include Easter eggs available in Gold Brick, Heavenly Hash, Assorted Cremes, Peanut Butter, and Pecan.

The Elmer Candy Corporation was purchased by the Nelson family in 1965. The name Elmer was retained because Elmer's tune in terms of confectionery items still is a familiar melody not only in the South, but in all other parts of the country.

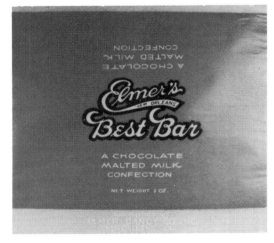

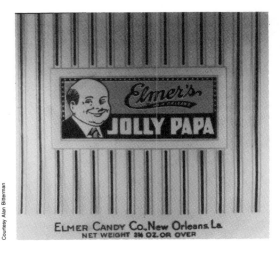

II

Recipes and Staying Trim

The Making of Chocolate

What has made the candy bar such a favorite of the American palate over the years? Chocolate. Approximately 70 percent of the candy bars now produced are chocolate covered. Many other bars include chocolate as one of the ingredients.

The cacao tree, *Theobroma cacao*, grows chiefly in West Africa, Brazil, Ecuador, Venezuela, and the Indies. It is a short, leafy tree reaching a height of fifteen to twenty feet. After harvest, the pods containing the beans are cut open. The cacao beans are fermented and dried, then bagged and shipped.

On arrival at the chocolate factory, the beans are thoroughly cleaned and then roasted at controlled temperatures. The roasting brings out the full flavor and aroma of the beans. After roasting, the outer shells are removed, leaving the nib, the meat part of the bean.

The nibs are ground in huge stone mills, which produces heat. As a result, the nibs (which contain 53 to 56 percent cocoa butter) melt. The resulting liquid becomes what is known as *chocolate liquor*. When it is cooled and molded into bars, it becomes unsweetened or cooking chocolate.

Cocoa butter is the natural fat of the cocoa bean, and it has a delicate chocolate aroma. Huge hydraulic presses are used to remove it from chocolate liquor. The cocoa butter is used to give body, smoothness, and flavor to eating chocolate.

After the cocoa butter has been pressed out of the chocolate liquor, a "press cake" remains. This cake is ground and sifted, becoming cocoa powder. Natural cocoa powder has a lighter color than does Dutch cocoa powder, which is neutralized for a darker color and different flavor.

To make what is known as semi-sweet (or vanilla) chocolate, cocoa butter, sugar, and vanilla flavoring are added to the chocolate liquor. After thorough blending, the mixture is refined for smoothness and then conched, a process in which flavor is developed.

Conching is a two- to four-day kneading process, done at high temperatures. After being conched, the chocolate is tempered by being stirred vigorously while it is heated, cooled, and then heated again. After tempering, the finished sweet chocolate is cooled and molded into bars, which are dark in color. The vanilla added only imparts flavor—it doesn't lighten the color.

Milk chocolate is made in a similar fashion to semi-sweet (vanilla) chocolate, except that whole milk replaces some of the chocolate liquor in the blend. The water in the milk is removed during the processing, and the milk solid imparts a lightened color to the resulting chocolate blend.

By law, real chocolate includes chocolate liquor and cocoa butter. Chocolate-flavored confectionery coatings are basically sweetened combinations of cocoa powder and vegetable fats other than cocoa butter.

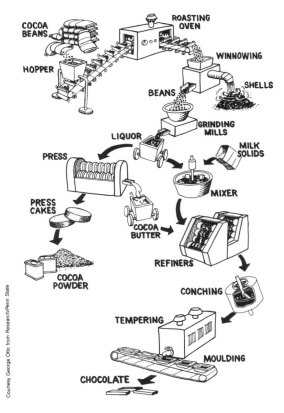

Courtesy George Otto from Research/Penn State

The Making of a Candy Bar

What do *The Wall Street Journal* and Dolly Parton have in common? In December 1982, *The Wall Street Journal* carried a front-page article about the candy bar Goo Goo Cluster. A year later, in December 1983, Dolly Parton gave several hundred Goo Goos to Hollywood friends at her Christmas party.

Who makes the Goo Goo? The Standard Candy Company in Nashville, Tennessee. And nicer folks you'd never meet than the Goo Goo people. If you're ever in Nashville, make arrangements with the plant for a free tour of the facilities. Standard is one of the confectionery companies that still offers public tours (with tasty treats available at the end of the line, too).

The Goo Goo Cluster has been around since 1912. Standard's Chocolate Cocoanut Creme bar, no longer being made, was a popular seller in the 1920s and 1930s. Introduced in 1982 was a companion bar to the Goo Goo Cluster, the Goo Goo Supreme. It has the Goo Goo's same smooth, creamy marshmallow, rich, luscious caramel, and the same milk chocolate. The difference between the Goo Goo Cluster and the Goo Goo Supreme is the peanuts in the Cluster. The Supreme has pecans and a tad more milk chocolate.

Ready to take a picture tour of the steps in making a Goo Goo Cluster?

The spacious refrigerated storeroom holds incoming ingredients for all Standard products. It is also used to maintain freshness of finished products until they are shipped out to neighborhood stores.

Shelled Georgia peanuts are prepared for inspection by being poured into a hopper, where they drop onto a conveyor belt. The peanuts are inspected and, if not rejected, are sent into the roasting process.

The ingredients used for Goo Goo Cluster centers of caramel and marshmallow are produced daily in the kitchen above the tray room. The ingredients from the kitchen flow through funnels and are deposited in circular depressions

in the cornstarch carried in wooden trays. The filled trays are then stored on dollies in a moisture-controlled aging room until the centers are properly cured.

The peanuts have been inspected and roasted, the caramel and marshmallow have been aged, the pure milk chocolate has been tempered and is in liquid form. Now it's time to combine these ingredients into Goo Goo Clusters. The caramel-marshmallow centers are placed caramel side up in little basket containers riding on a conveyor belt.

As the rows of centers in their baskets pass underneath the peanut hopper, peanuts are deposited on the centers. The conveyor belt then carries the centers and peanuts through a chocolate enrober.

The now chocolate-covered Goo Goo Clusters enter a long cooling tunnel. The Goo Goos move slowly through the refrigeration process to solidify the chocolate and ensure a polished sheen. As the bars, nine in a row, come out of the cooling tunnel, each finished bar is carefully inspected for quality control. The bars passing inspection now move single file on a conveyor belt through an automatic wrapping machine.

The machine-wrapped Goo Goos are now hand packed into boxes. From there, they are conveyed to be packed into shipping boxes. Finally, the shipping boxes are moved to the refrigerated storeroom until they are sent to stores.

Now it's time to taste and enjoy a Goo Goo Cluster! Tour's over.

Bars and Books

One of the most respected confectioners in the early candy bar years was George Williamson of Chicago. He, along with Otto Schnering of the Curtiss Candy Company, made national advertising work for candy bars.

George Williamson's Oh Henry! became a success nationwide in the 1920s because of Williamson's effective use of ads in such publications as *The American Magazine, The Saturday Evening Post, Good Housekeeping, Ladies' Home Journal, The Delineator, Pictorial Review,* and *The American Boy.*

Williamson, creative in more ways than one, conceived of using Oh Henry! candy bars in dessert recipes. Women were asked to send in their favorite recipes, and in less than two months, more than eight thousand recipes poured in for the use of Oh Henry! candy bars not only in desserts such as cakes, icings, pudding, ice cream, and baked apples, but also for such dishes as toast and salads. The best recipes were then used in a recipe book, published in 1926, called *60 New Ways To Serve a Famous Candy*.

Cake and Cake Icing

OH HENRY! CAKE FROSTING
Originated by Mrs. Frank R. Rousseau, Grand Isle, Vt.

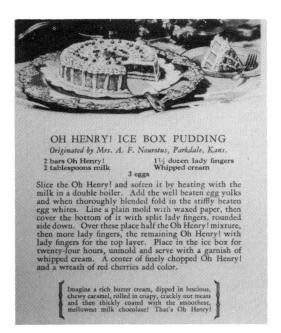

OH HENRY! ICE BOX PUDDING
Originated by Mrs. A. F. Nourotus, Parkdale, Kans.

2 bars Oh Henry! 1½ dozen lady fingers
2 tablespoons milk Whipped cream
3 eggs

Slice the Oh Henry! and soften it by heating with the milk in a double boiler. Add the well beaten egg yolks and when thoroughly blended fold in the stiffly beaten egg whites. Line a plain mold with waxed paper, then cover the bottom of it with split lady fingers, rounded side down. Over these place half the Oh Henry! mixture, then more lady fingers, the remaining Oh Henry! with lady fingers for the top layer. Place in the ice box for twenty-four hours, unmold and serve with a garnish of whipped cream. A center of finely chopped Oh Henry! and a wreath of red cherries add color.

[Imagine a rich butter cream, dipped in luscious, chewy caramel, rolled in crispy, crackly nut meats and then thickly coated with the smoothest, mellowest milk chocolate! That's Oh Henry!]

Free copies were available from the Williamson Candy Company. The Foreword to the book said:

> A young society matron of Chicago, entertaining at bridge, found she had forgotten to order chocolates! In her dilemma she hurriedly sliced some of her brother's reserve stock of Oh Henry! It looked attractive, so she served it. Relief was mingled with amusement at the flutter with which her guests welcomed this "new" bon bon.
>
> Quickly the idea "caught on." If Oh Henry! had pleased the universal taste in its bar form, when *sliced*, its goodness created little less than a furor. Everywhere, on every sort of occasion, women began serving Oh Henry!, sliced, as they had served chocolates.
>
> And then mothers began to realize that a candy with such appeal, and of such food value, was worthy of general use at home. They began to experiment in the kitchen, and they sent us recipes, recipes, recipes!

Some of the more exotic recipes in the book were Oh Henry! Stuffed Tomatoes, Oh Henry! Sticky Buns, Oh Henry! Tutti Fruitti Ice Cream, Oh Henry! Surprise Pie, and Ozark Birthday Cake.

Without a doubt, Williamson's candy bar book was one of the hits of 1926. As a result, the company began charging ten cents (in "stamps or silver") for each copy.

Today, sixty years after the publication

of the forty-page book, copies are to be found only in the hands of a few collectors. The spirit of George Williamson's advertising creativity lingers on.

Reproduced here are the book's introduction and some of the recipes. Keep in mind that in 1926, Oh Henry! weighed about three ounces, and that the recipes were not developed under modern kitchen conditions.

How to Prepare Oh Henry! for Using in Cooking

In the recipes which follow, Oh Henry! is sometimes used sliced, sometimes diced, sometimes chopped or melted.

It will be found very easy to slice if a short and fairly good-sized knife is used. Place the middle of the blade on the bar and exert an even pressure, having both hands on the knife, one at either side of the bar. In this way smooth, even slices are easily cut.

To dice Oh Henry!, first cut it into slices one-third inch thick, lay these flat on the wrapper or board and cut crosswise into dices of the desired size.

It will sometimes be found that a few irregular pieces break off in slicing or dicing Oh Henry! It is a good plan to save these for use in recipes where chopped Oh Henry! is called for. In fact, all left-over pieces of Oh Henry! can be saved for such a purpose in a covered jar. It keeps well in the pantry.

To melt Oh Henry! first cut it into slices. Place in a heavy saucepan, set over a gentle heat and allow the Oh Henry! to soften. If to be used with other ingredients for a sauce or a frosting, place the necessary amount of Oh Henry! in the inner vessel of a double boiler, with a little cream, milk or water—from one to three tablespoons for each bar according to the consistency desired.

Don't grind Oh Henry! This breaks up the nuts and for many uses destroys the uniquely delicious Oh Henry! flavor.

Don't add too much sugar. Remember that there is a large percentage of sugar in Oh Henry! itself. Too much added would give an over-sweetness.

Don't be afraid to use enough Oh Henry! whether eaten as a candy or used in preparing cooked dishes. Every ingredient is most carefully selected and of the utmost purity, making Oh Henry! rich in nutritive value as well as rich in flavor.

Fried Bananas with Oh Henry! Dressing

6	bananas
3	tablespoons butter
2	tablespoons sugar
1	teaspoon lemon juice
2	bars Oh Henry!
2	tablespoons heavy cream

Split the bananas and cook them in the butter, turning so as to brown both sides. Place on a serving dish, sprinkle with the sugar, and squeeze the lemon juice over. Cover with a dressing made by melting the Oh Henry! with the cream and a tablespoon of butter, using any left over from cooking the bananas and adding more if needed.

Oh Henry! Stuffed Tomatoes

2	bars Oh Henry!
3	medium-sized tomatoes
2	tablespoons mayonnaise
⅓	teaspoon salt
	lettuce

Cut the Oh Henry! into small pieces. Remove the skins from the tomatoes, cut a slice from the top of each and carefully hollow out the centers. Dice these, drain off all the liquid, add the Oh Henry!, blend with the mayonnaise and salt, and use to refill the tomato shells. Chill and serve on lettuce.

Toasted Oh Henry! Marshmallows

marshmallows
Oh Henry!

Cut the marshmallows crosswise into halves with sharp scissors and place a thin slice of Oh Henry! between the halves, sandwich wise. (It may be necessary to press the marshmallows between thumb and fingers a little to make them large enough to inclose the slice of Oh Henry!) Toast quickly and serve at once.

Oh Henry! Surprise Pie

Cut Oh Henry! into thin slices and lay these close together on a previously cooked custard, butterscotch, cream or similar pie, then cover with meringue and return to a cool oven to set and delicately color the meringue. The Oh Henry! will slightly melt, thus forming a delicious layer over the pie filling.

Chocolate Birthday Cake with Oh Henry! Filling

Part 1

1	cup brown sugar
1	cup grated chocolate
½	cup hot coffee

Place all three ingredients in the inner vessel of the double boiler. Heat until the chocolate and sugar are dissolved but do not let the mixture boil. When cool stir into Part 2.

Part 2

1	cup brown sugar
½	cup butter
3	eggs
½	cup coffee
2	cups flour
1	teaspoon lemon extract
1	teaspoon vanilla extract
¼	teaspoon salt
1	teaspoon soda
2	teaspoons baking soda

Beat the sugar and butter together until light. Add the eggs, well beaten, the coffee, flavoring extracts, then the mixture prepared as for Part 1, and lastly the flour, salt, soda and baking powder sifted together. Bake in two large layer cake pans and put together with Oh Henry! filling. (See below.)

Oh Henry! Cake Filling

1½	cups granulated sugar
½	cup water
	pinch of cream of tartar
2	egg whites
2	bars Oh Henry!

Boil the sugar, water and cream of tartar together without stirring, to the soft ball stage—if using thermometer cook to 238 degrees F. Pour slowly over the stiffly beaten egg whites, beating constantly while pouring. Have the Oh Henry! shaved finely, then cut into small pieces. Add to the filling while still hot, and spread quickly.

CHOCOLATE BIRTHDAY CAKE
WITH OH HENRY! FILLING
Originated by Miss L. O. B., Eureka Springs, Ark.

Oh Henry! Marguerites

small saltines
Oh Henry!
marshmallows

Lay the saltines side by side on a baking pan, place thinly sliced Oh Henry! on each and cover with marshmallows which have been split crosswise. Bake in a moderate oven—375 degrees F.—until the marshmallows are golden brown, tender and puffy. Serve immediately.

TEA DAINTIES

OH HENRY! MARGUERITES

Oh Henry! Toast for Afternoon Tea

4   thin slices white bread
     butter
1   bar Oh Henry!

Toast the bread golden brown, remove the crusts, butter, cut each slice into halves, then lay on each piece very thin slices of Oh Henry! allowing these to almost touch. Place in a hot oven— 375-400 degrees F.—for from three to four minutes to allow Oh Henry! to heat and soften. Serve at once.

OH HENRY! TOAST
FOR AFTERNOON TEA

Oh Henry! with Toasted Cheese

     soda crackers
     grated cheese
     thin slices of Oh Henry!

Place soda crackers close together in a flat baking pan. Cover them thickly with grated cheese and place a thin slice of Oh Henry! in the center of each cracker. Bake in a moderately hot oven until the cheese is slightly browned and the Oh Henry! begins to melt. Serve immediately.

Oh Henry! Fritters

1   cup flour
1   teaspoon baking powder
⅙   teaspoon salt
1   egg
     about ½ cup milk
1   bar Oh Henry! sliced

Sift together the flour, baking powder and salt; add the egg yolk and milk and mix until smooth, beating out all lumps. Beat the egg white until stiff and fold it gently into the batter. Use to coat slices of Oh Henry!, frying these in deep fat or sautéing and turning when brown on one side. Serve with a sweet liquid sauce.

Oh Henry! Stuffed Dates

     dates
     Oh Henry!
     granulated sugar

Cut Oh Henry! into quarter inch slices, divide these crosswise into halves, warm slightly by placing in a bowl set over hot water and mold with the hands into small rolls. Use these to fill dates from which the stones have been removed, then roll each date in granulated sugar.

Oh Henry! Molasses Cakes

½   cup shortening
½   cup sugar
1   egg
     grated rind ½ orange
3   cups flour
¼   teaspoon salt
1   teaspoon soda
1   teaspoon ground cinnamon
½   teaspoon ground cloves
1   cup boiling water
1   teaspoon ground ginger

Cream the shortening and sugar; add the well beaten egg, molasses, and grated orange rind; then the flour, salt, soda and spices thoroughly sifted together. Pour the boiling water over the ginger and add last. Beat well and bake in well greased cup cake pans in a moderate oven 350–375 degrees F. about twenty minutes. Shortly before removing from the oven put two thin slices of Oh Henry! on each cake and return to the oven for a moment to melt as a frosting.

OH HENRY! MOLASSES CAKES

Oh Henry! Rosettes
leftover pastry
diced Oh Henry!

Use for the Rosettes the trimmings left over after making pies. Roll thinly and spread generously with the Oh Henry! Wet the edges of the pastry, roll up like a jelly roll and cut into thick slices. Place these cut sides up and down on a well greased baking sheet and bake about fifteen minutes in a moderate oven—375 degrees F. Remove from the pan as soon as baked and serve immediately.

❧ ❧ PASTRY ❧ ❧

Oh Henry! Stuffed Baked Apples
6	apples
1	cup water
1½	bars Oh Henry!
1	cup brown sugar

Wash and core the apples, place them in a shallow saucepan and simmer gently for ten minutes; then place in a buttered baking dish and fill the centers with Oh Henry! allowing for each apple a quarter of a bar sliced length-wise then crosswise. Add the sugar to the water in which the apples were simmered, boil these together for a moment, then pour into the dish around the apples. Bake in a moderate oven— 350 to 375 degrees F. —about twenty minutes.

OH HENRY! STUFFED BAKED APPLES

Oh Henry! Guest Pudding
1	package prepared table jelly
1	bar Oh Henry! diced
1	pint boiling water
	whipped cream

Dissolve the jelly in the boiling water and set aside until almost set, then stir in the diced Oh Henry! and turn into one large or several individual molds which have been dipped into cold water. Chill, unmold and serve with whipped cream flavored with vanilla.

Any preferred jelly flavor may be used, chocolate or cherry being particularly good.

OH HENRY! GUEST PUDDING

Oh Henry! Sticky Buns

2	cups flour
4	teaspoons baking powder
1/3	teaspoon salt
2	tablespoons shortening
	about 2/3 cup milk
	a little softened butter
1/2	cup brown sugar
3	bars Oh Henry! sliced

Sift together the flour, baking powder and salt; rub in the shortening and mix to a light dough with the milk. Roll out thinly, spread with the softened butter and sprinkle half the sugar over this. Cover with half the slices of Oh Henry!, roll up, and cut into slices about an inch thick. Butter a baking pan; sprinkle over it the remaining sugar; cover with the remaining Oh Henry!, then place on this the rolled dough. Bake in a moderate oven—375 degrees F. — from fifteen to twenty minutes. When done turn out immediately by inverting the pan so that the melted Oh Henry! is now on top forming a sticky coating on the buns.

Fruit Salad with Oh Henry!

1	cup skinned seeded Malaga grapes or white cherries
1	cup diced orange, freed from pith and seeds
1	cup diced fresh or canned pineapple
1	bar Oh Henry! (shaved)
1/2	cup whipped cream
1/2	cup mayonnaise
	lettuce

Prepare and blend the fruits. Place in a cloth or strainer and drain, then chill. Just before serving add the blended whipped cream and mayonnaise and two-thirds of the Oh Henry! Serve on lettuce, and sprinkle the remaining shaved Oh Henry! over the top.

FRUIT SALAD WITH OH HENRY!

Oh Henry! Filled Doughnuts

Use any preferred doughnut recipe, mixing as usual and rolling out thinly. Cut into rounds with a biscuit cutter; wet the edges of half the rounds with water; put a slice of Oh Henry! on each of these and cover with the remaining rounds of dough, pressing the edges very firmly together. Then fry as usual in deep hot fat.

These are delicious but do not keep well when there are boys in the family!

Oh Henry! Surprise Popcorn Balls

Over three quarts of popped corn (measured after popping) pour one cupful of molasses which has been boiled for twelve minutes. Stir briskly until thoroughly mixed with the corn. While still warm, and with oiled hands, shape around slices of Oh Henry! into balls of the desired size. Roll each ball in a square of waxed paper when cold.

Baby Ruth Time

During World War II, the Curtiss Candy Company featured a cookie recipe using Baby Ruth bars. Advertisements were carried in national publications such as *Good Housekeeping* in 1942. The ads indicated that servicemen and women would appreciate cookies from home made the Baby Ruth way. And besides, three cookies could be made at a cost of a penny or less.

The Baby Ruth candy bar wrapper produced in 1942 carried the same recipe, but the ingredient amounts were slightly different on the wrapper than on the ad. The wrapper recipe, shown below, was easier to follow. At the time, a Baby Ruth weighed one and one-quarter ounces.

Baby Ruth Cookies

1	egg
1⅓	cups flour
½	teaspoon salt
¾	cup white sugar
½	teaspoon soda
½	teaspoon vanilla
½	cup butter, or other shortening
2	Curtiss 5¢ Baby Ruth bars, cut in small pieces

Cream butter and sugar until smooth. Beat in egg. Stir in other ingredients. Chill and drop by half teaspoon on greased cookie sheet. Bake in a moderately hot oven (375°F).

The cookies were indeed tasty and certainly deserve duplication today. The concept of using candy bars instead of chocolate chips in cookies is refreshing, considering that everyone and their uncle, especially on the commercial level under various trade names, seems to be producing the ultimate in chocolate chip cookies these days.

Try the recipe with your favorite candy bar. Who knows? You might come up with a real winner in your kitchen. Be careful if you go commercial though. Don't infringe on the use of a trade name,

and don't forget that Baby Ruth Cookies were a product of 1940s kitchen technology—not today's.

Delicious. . .Homemade!

In the 1950s, the Welch Candy Company (now a part of Nabisco), advertised frequently in magazines such as *Life* and

Saturday Evening Post. Often featured were Welch's Cocoanut Candy Bars. In some of those ads, Welch's went so far as to provide special recipes for making chocolate covered cocoanut bars! Here's a recipe for that bar as it appeared in *Life*, September 1950.

Chocolate Covered Cocoanut Bars

1	cup packaged, sweetened moist cocoanut (chopped fine)
2	cups granulated sugar
¾	cup fresh sweet milk
1	tablespoon light corn syrup
1	tablespoon dairy fresh butter
1	teaspoon vanilla
2	tablespoons marshmallow
⅛	teaspoon salt
1	lb. semi-sweet chocolate

Stir sugar, corn syrup and milk in saucepan over fire till dissolved. Cover and cook to medium soft ball (240°F). Remove from heat and add butter, stirring only enough to blend. Pour on cold wet platter. When luke-warm (110°F) beat with spatula until thick and creamy. Mix in salt, vanilla, and marshmallow. Knead in cocoanut and form into bars. When cool, cover with melted semi-sweet chocolate. Makes 16 bars.

Choice Recipes

In 1926, many booklets provided recipes with candy ingredients. A prize collector's item today is the Walter Baker and Company, Ltd., booklet, *Choice Recipes*. The 1926 edition contained recipes for using chocolate or cocoa in beverages, cakes, icings and fillings, sauces, and hot and cold desserts. Also included was a section on frozen desserts, which explained how to use a mixture of three parts finely crushed ice to one part rock salt for freezing.

The booklet contained a section of miscellaneous recipes, recipes for children and invalids, and candy recipes prepared by a Mrs. Janet McKenzie Hill. In addition, the booklet pictured the finished goodies in full color.

Three of the candy recipes were named after leading women's colleges, so the recipes themselves had a certain prestige. These three recipes are reproduced from Baker's 1926 booklet.

Vassar Fudge

2   cups granulated sugar
1   tablespoon butter
1   cup cream or evaporated milk
4   ounces Baker's Premium
      No. 1 Chocolate

Mix the sugar and cream and stir until sugar dissolves. Add the chocolate broken into fine pieces. Stir constantly until boiling, then put in butter. Boil until a little of the mixture will form a soft ball when dropped in cold water. Remove and beat until quite cool and thick. Pour into buttered tin. When cold, cut in diamond-shaped pieces.

PEPPERMINTS, CHOCOLATE MINTS, ETC. (See Page 40.)

CHOCOLATE DIPPED PARISIAN SWEETS (See Page 44.)

VASSAR FUDGE (See Page 50.)

GINGER, CHERRY, APRICOT AND NUT CHOCOLATES. (See Page 41.)

CHOCOLATE COCOANUT CAKES. (See Page 52.)

CHOCOLATE NUT CARAMELS. (See Page 54.)

ALMOND AND CHERRY CHOCOLATE CREAMS

Smith College Fudge

Melt one-quarter cup butter. Mix together one cup white sugar, one cup brown sugar, one-quarter cup molasses and one-half cup cream or evaporated milk. Add this to the butter and heat to boiling point. Boil for two and one-half minutes, stirring rapidly. Then add two ounces of Baker's Premium No. 1 Chocolate, cut fine. Boil five minutes stirring rapidly at first and then more slowly towards the end. Remove from the fire, add one and one-half teaspoons vanilla. Then stir constantly until the mass thickens. Pour into buttered pan and set in a cool place to harden.

RIBBON CARAMELS.
(See Page 54.)

ALMOND FONDANT BALLS.
(See Page 48.)

DOUBLE FUDGE.
(See Page 50.)

ROSE AND PISTACHIO
CHOCOLATE CREAMS.
(See Pages 43 & 49.)

WALNUT CREAM CHOCOLATES.
(See Page 48.)

ALMOND FONDANT STICKS.
(See Page 47.)

SMITH COLLEGE FUDGE.

Wellesley Marshmallow Fudge

Heat two cups granulated sugar and one cup rich milk or cream until sugar dissolves. Add two ounces Baker's Premium No. 1 Chocolate and boil until it hardens in cold water. Just before it is done, add one or two tablespoons of butter, then remove from the fire and begin to stir in half a pound of marshmallows, crushing and beating them with a spoon and adding a few at a time. Pour into a buttered pan three-quarters of an inch thick, cool and cut into cubes.

The Baker's booklet also contained several recipes for making homemade candy in bar shape, including these Chocolate Almond Bars and Almond Fondant Sticks.

Chocolate Almond Bars

½   cup sugar
¾   cup white corn syrup
½   cup water
½   cup blanched almonds, chopped fine
1½   cups fondant
3   or 4 ounces Baker's Premium No. 1 Chocolate
1   teaspoon vanilla

Melt the sugar in the water and corn syrup and let boil to 252°F., or between a soft and a hard ball. Add the almonds and the vanilla, mix thoroughly and turn onto a marble slab or a platter over which powdered sugar has been sifted.

Turn out the candy in such a way that it will take a rectangular shape on marble. When cool enough, make it in strips about an inch and a quarter wide, and, as it grows cooler, lift the strips, one by one, to a board and cut them in pieces half or three-quarters of an inch wide. When cold, drop them, sugar side down, in fondant mixed with the chocolate and prepared for dipping. With the fork, push them below the fondant, lift out, drain as much as possible, and set onto oilcloth, waxed paper or a marble slab. These improve upon keeping.

Almond Fondant Sticks

2½   cups confectioner's or granulated sugar
¼   cup white corn syrup
½   cup water
¼   pound almond paste
¼   pound Baker's Premium No. 1 Chocolate

1   teaspoon vanilla extract
½   pound Baker's "Dot" Chocolate

Put the sugar, corn syrup, and water over the fire. Stir until the sugar is dissolved. Wash down the sides of the kettle as in making fondant. Let boil to a soft ball degree or to 238°F. Add the almond paste cut into small thin pieces, let boil up vigorously, then turn onto a damp marble slab or a large platter. When nearly cold, work to a cream with wooden spatula. It will take considerable time to turn this mixture to fondant. Cover and let stand half an hour. Add the chocolate melted over hot water, and the vanilla, and knead thoroughly. The chocolate must be added warm. At once, cut off a portion of the fondant and knead it into a round ball; then roll it lightly under the fingers into a long strip the shape and size of a lead pencil; form as many of these strips as desired; cut the strips into two-inch lengths and let stand to become firm. Dip in melted "Dot" Chocolate.

The index to the booklet listed the names of the recipes' creators, including Miss Parloa, Miss Robinson, Mrs. Ewing, Mrs. Andrea, and Miss Farmer. Chances are that the Miss Farmer listed was Fannie Merrit Farmer, who had made a name for herself in cookery.

The delightful *Choice Recipes* was certainly one of the highlights of 1926 for those who enjoyed making and eating chocolate and cocoa treats.

Making Your Own

Gloria Pitzer bills herself as "The Recipe Detective." Over the years, she has found a calling for imitating the "secret recipes" of the food industry and has come up with more than two thousand published recipes for all kinds of food, including candy bars.

A syndicated newspaper columnist, Pitzer eventually found it satisfying to produce her own paper, *Secret Recipe Report*. Then she began publishing her own recipe books. Here are some of her candy bar and candy recipes, each of which imitates a commercially produced product you'll be able to recognize.

Gloria Pitzer's
Recess Peanut Butter Cups
1   8-ounce bar Hershey Milk Chocolate
1½   cups peanut butter
4   tablespoons butter or margarine

In top of double boiler over HOT, not boiling water, melt chocolate with HALF of the peanut butter. Stir till smooth. Put remaining half of peanut butter in top of another double boiler over simmering water (or put it into a heat-proof bowl and set that in a shallow pan of simmering water). Let the peanut butter melt just till it is of a pouring consistency. Have 24 miniature muffin paper liners placed inside cupcake or muffin tin wells. You can place them side-by-side on a cookie sheet, but I like the support that the cup- cake tin wells give the papers while the candy is "setting." Next you divide HALF of the chocolate mix- ture, equally between each of the paper liners.

Then divide ALL of the melted peanut butter between them over the chocolate and finally divide the remaining chocolate over the peanut butter. You have now the bottom layer of chocolate, then the peanut butter, and finally the top layer of chocolate.

Let these stand at room tempera- ture about 2 hours to "set." Keep them refrigerated in a covered con- tainer up to a week, or freeze them, individually wrapped in waxed paper or a sandwich-sized plastic food bag. They will keep frozen for months and months . . . but they won't last that long.

NOTE: If you don't want to bother with the cups, grease a 9″ square pan, spreading half of the chocolate mixture evenly over the bottom of that and then the peanut butter evenly over that and finally spread the remaining chocolate mixture over the peanut butter layer. Let it "set" till firm to the touch and cut into neat little squares. Makes 36 pieces. (The addition of 6 tablespoons of melted paraffin is optional, but I do use it, adding it to the chocolate when I melt it with the peanut butter. It's up to you!)

Gloria Pitzer's
Shallow Cup Marshmallow Candies

In top of double boiler over gently simmering water, melt 8-ounce bar Hershey Milk Chocolate with 4 tablespoons butter, ½ cup of a 7-ounce jar of marshmallow creme. Stir till smooth. Put 1 cup flaked coconut on an ungreased cookie

sheet into a 375ºF. oven till lightly browned. Stir coconut frequently to brown it evenly. Cool it and crush it fine with rolling pin. Stir it into chocolate mixture. Place rest of that jar of marshmallow creme in a heat- proof bowl. Place in a pan of sim- mering water till it is of a "pouring" consistency. Divide half of the chocolate mixture between 24 minia- ture muffin paper liners. Divide the marshmallow equally over that and then divide remaining chocolate over the top. Chill till firm or "set." Makes about 2 dozen candy cups.

NOTE: Pan Sized Mallow Squares—rather than fuss with the paper liners and such, make a quick job of it by altering the shapes, sim- ply taking half of the chocolate mix- ture and spreading it evenly over bottom of buttered 9″ square pan. Then pour the warm marshmallow creme over that and as soon as the creme has "set" a bit, spread remaining half of chocolate over that. Let it stand at room tempera- ture about an hour. Then cut into squares. Makes about 24 squares.

Gloria Pitzer's
English Toffee—*Teeth Bars*

1	cup butter
1	cup sugar
¼	cup water
½	teaspoon salt
3	ounces semi-sweet chocolate
	(⅔ cup chocolate chips)

Combine butter, sugar, water, salt in heavy 2½-quart saucepan over medium heat. Stir constantly till mixture reaches 300ºF. —or a small amount dropped into glass of cold water "cracks" when it hits the water (called "Hard Crack Stage"). This you must really watch carefully or it will scorch. Takes only 20 or 30 seconds for it to go from just right to uugghhh . . . . At once pour into UNGREASED 9″ x 13″ x 2″ pan.

Let it cool about 2 hours or till hard to the touch. Melt chocolate over HOT not boiling water and spread over the hardened candy. Invert pan onto working surface where you can break it up into bite sized pieces. OR while toffee is beginning to cool and is a bit tacky when you touch it, you can oil a pancake turner and score the toffee into bars. These should break apart quite easily then. Rather than invert the pan when candy is cool, lift up one corner with a spatula and the entire toffee should lift right out of the pan, so that you can snap the scored portions apart. Makes about 1 pound.

Gloria Pitzer's *Life Slivers*— The Candy WITHOUT the Holes

- 3¾ cup sugar
- 1½ cups light corn syrup
- 1 cup water
- 1 teaspoon flavoring oil of your choice (this is not extract but an oil from the pharmacy)
- 6 or 8 drops assorted food coloring

Mix together sugar, corn syrup, water in heavy 2½-quart saucepan. Cook on medium heat, stirring constantly. Bring to boil. Boil without stirring till it reaches 310°F.—a bit more than "hard crack" stage—or when a few drops from a spoon of the hot candy into cold water causes candy to make a "cracking" sound. Remove then from heat. Add flavoring oil and food coloring. Pour onto foil-lined pans or cookie sheets so that it is about 1/8" thick. When candy hardens at room temperature (within an hour), you can break it into slivers and dust in powdered sugar. Store ,at room temperature in covered container. Makes 2 pounds.

Gloria Pitzer's *Pater Paul Ounce Bars*

Combine ½ pound butter or margarine, 14-ounce can Eagle Brand Milk, 1 teaspoon vanilla, mixing well. Cover and refrigerate 4 hours. Beat into it at that time, two pounds powdered sugar, a little at a time till quite stiff in texture. Work in 2 packages (7-ounces each) flaked coconut. Pat firmly into bottom of greased jelly roll pan or 2 greased 9" x 13" x 2" pans. Chill till firm. Cut into 2" x 1" bars. Over simmering water melt 12 ounces semi-sweet chocolate chips and 4 ounces Nestlé's Milk Chocolate with 3 tablespoons melted paraffin till smooth. Spear each bar with tip of knife. Dip to coat in warm chocolate, letting excess drip back into pan. Air dry. Store at room temperature in covered containers for weeks and weeks. Keep away from humidity or steam from cooking utensils and appliances.

NOTE: The preceding Gloria Pitzer recipes reprinted with permission from Secret Recipes, Box 152, St. Clair, Michigan 48079.

The Nestlé Way

The folks at Nestlé share the following up-to-date, tested recipes that can be done at home.

100 Grand Recipe

- 4 1.6-oz. Nestlé 100 Grand bars
- 1 cup miniature marshmallows (or 8 large marshmallows)
- ¼ cup butter
- 2 cups oven-toasted rice-cereal

Combine over hot (not boiling) water, Nestlé 100 Grand bars, marshmallows and butter; heat until chocolate and marshmallows melt and mixture is well blended. Remove from heat. Stir in cereal. Press into aluminum foil-lined 8″ square pan. Chill in refrigerator until firm (about 2 hours). Cut into 1″ squares. Makes sixty-four 1″ squares.

S'mores

4	⅛ oz. Nestlé chocolate bars, cut in half crosswise
4	graham crackers, cut in half crosswise
4	large marshmallows

Using conventional oven: Preheat oven to 350°F. For each S'more place one half of Nestlé Milk Chocolate bar on half of graham cracker. Top with a marshmallow. Place on ungreased cookie sheet. Bake at 350°F. for 5-7 minutes. Remove from oven. Top with second half of chocolate bar and graham cracker. Gently press together. Makes four 2½″ sandwich cookies.

Using microwave oven: For each S'more, place one half of Nestlé chocolate bar on half of graham cracker. Top with marshmallow. Place in a circle on plastic or paper plate. Cook in microwave oven on medium for 10–15 seconds or until soft. Top with second half of chocolate bar and graham cracker. Gently press together. Makes four 2½″ sandwich cookies.

ChocoNut Caramel Bars

1	11½-oz. pkg (2 cups) Nestlé Milk Chocolate Morsels
2	measuring tablespoons vegetable shortening
30	vanilla caramels
3	measuring tablespoons butter
2	measuring tablespoons water
1	cup coarsely chopped peanuts

Melt over hot (not boiling) water, Nestlé Milk Chocolate Morsels and vegetable shortening. Stir until morsels melt and mixture is smooth. Remove from heat. Pour ½ of melted chocolate into an 8″ foil-lined square pan; spread evenly. Refrigerate until

firm (about 15 minutes). Return remaining chocolate mixture to *low* heat. Combine over boiling water, caramels, butter, and water. Stir until caramels melt and mixture is smooth. Stir in nuts until well blended. Pour into the chocolate-lined pan. Spread evenly. Refrigerate until tacky, about 15 minutes. Top with remaining melted chocolate, spread evenly to cover caramel filling. Return to refrigerator and chill until firm (about 1 hour).

Cut into 1″ x 2″ rectangles. Refrigerate until ready to serve. Makes about 2½ dozen candies.

Peanut Fudge Log

½	cup chunky peanut butter
1	measuring tablespoon butter or margarine, softened
2	measuring tablespoons sifted confectioners' sugar
1	measuring tablespoon orange juice
1	measuring teaspoon orange rind
1	measuring teaspoon vanilla extract
½	cup chopped nuts
½	cup chopped raisins
1	11½ oz. pkg. (2 cups) Nestlé Milk Chocolate Morsels
½	cup sweetened condensed milk (not evaporated milk)
⅛	measuring teaspoon salt
½	measuring teaspoon vanilla extract
	(Logs may be frozen up to 1 month)

In small bowl, combine peanut butter, butter or margarine, confectioners' sugar, orange juice, orange rind and 1 measuring teaspoon vanilla extract. Beat until well blended. Add nuts and raisins; mix well. Roll into two 10″ logs; set aside. Melt over hot (not boiling) water, Nestlé Milk Chocolate Morsels, sweetened condensed milk and salt. Heat until morsels melt and mixture is smooth. Remove from heat; add ½ measuring teaspoon vanilla extract. Pat ½ of mixture into 10″ x 3½″ oblong. Place 1 log in center of oblong; roll up and seal seam. Repeat for second log. Wrap in waxed paper. Chill until firm, about 1 hour. Cut into ¼″ slices. Preparation time, 35 minutes. Makes 80 candies.

Milk Chocolate Granola Bars

1   11½ oz. pkg. (2 cups) Nestlé Milk Chocolate Morsels
2   measuring tablespoons vegetable shortening
15   granola bars

Combine over hot (not boiling) water, Nestlé Milk Chocolate Morsels and vegetable shortening; heat until morsels melt and mixture is smooth. Coat granola bars with chocolate mixture. Place on waxed paper-lined cookie sheets. Chill in refrigerator until firm, about 30 minutes. Serve immediately or keep bars stored in refrigerator until ready to serve. Preparation time, 25 minutes. Makes 15 bars.

For chewier bars that tend to break, melt Nestlé Milk Chocolate Morsels and vegetable shortening over low heat in 10″ or 12″ heavy gauge skillet. Stir constantly until morsels melt and mixture is smooth. Dip as above. Use pancake turner to transfer bars to waxed paper-lined cookie sheet.

In 1956, the Nestlé Company ran an ad featuring a "New Idea! The chocolate bars you love best make a luscious easy treat." Though it hasn't been tested in today's kitchen, the recipe is included here for nostalgia's sake. The 1956 King Size bar was about eight ounces.

King Mallows

1. Melt over hot (not boiling) water, 2 Nestlé's King Size Chocolate Bars. Spread half the melted chocolate into a lightly greased pan, 8″ x 8″ x 2″.
2. Sprinkle 2 c. miniature marshmallows (or regular marshmallows, cut in eighths) over chocolate in pan. Spread remaining chocolate, gently, over marshmallows.
3. Chill before serving. Cut into squares. Yields approximately 1½ pounds. Your favorite Nestlé's bar—Milk, Crunch or Almond—will make your favorite kind of chocolate treat. Lots of fun to make—even more fun to eat. How about a King Mallows' party tonight?

Putting Goo Goos to Good Use

In the early 1980s, a privately owned ice cream shop in Nashville, Tennessee, created a Goo Goo Cluster ice cream recipe. Here's the recipe for Smith Brothers nifty ice cream treat.

Goo Goo Ice Cream

4	ounces unsweetened chocolate
8	tablespoons sugar
½	gallon half and half
3	eggs
1	pint whipping cream
1	pinch salt
2	ounces vanilla
6	Goo Goo Cluster bars, chopped

Dissolve chocolate and sugar in a double boiler with some of the half and half. Beat eggs, stir into above mixture and cook until slightly thickened.

Add remaining ingredients, except for the Goo Goos, stirring to combine. Pour into ice cream maker; freeze according to manufacturer's directions until mixture begins to firm up.

Add chopped Goo Goos and continue to freeze until desired consistency. Yields approximately 1½ gallons.

The folks in Nashville who make Goo Goos also make King Leo stick candy, and recipes have been developed for using that candy in a variety of ways.

King Leo Mint Pie

½	lb. King Leo Pure Mint Stick Candy
½	cup thin cream (half and half) chocolate wafers for crust
½	tablespoon plain gelatin
1	tablespoon cold water
1½	cups whipping cream

Crush Mint Sticks—add light or thin cream. Heat in double boiler until dissolved. Add gelatin which has been dissolved in 1 tablespoon cold water. Chill until partly set. Fold into whipping cream. Pour into crust made of chocolate wafers. Serve with whipped cream on top after chilling.

Fruit Salad Topping

Crumble King Leo Pure Peppermint Stick Candy for topping on your favorite fruit salad.

Iced Tea

Also try a stick of Peppermint or Lemon King Leo with a glass of iced tea—delightful and refreshing.

King Leo Mint Ice Cream

Dissolve twelve sticks of King Leo Pure Mint Sticks in one cup of milk in double boiler. Let cool. Add one pint of whipping cream which has already been whipped. Place in freezing tray, stirring occasionally.

Use above recipe for King Leo Pure Lemon Ice Cream, substituting 15 sticks of King Leo Pure Lemon Stick.

Mint Ice Cream is good when served with chocolate sauce.

Eating Candy Can Be Dandy

Nostalgia is defined as a longing for something long ago or for former happy circumstances, such a being a kid munching on a nickel candy bar without worrying about calories.

It probably wasn't until you became an adult that calories began to take on significance, especially if you were the kind of person prone to putting on weight. Chances are, sometime in your adult life, you were brainwashed by the thought that staying lean and mean meant eliminating pleasurable foods.

That thought, I'm pleased to say, really isn't on target. Eating should be both an enjoyable and sensible experience—even when you want to take off weight.

Thanks to the National Confectioners Association, a registered dietitian has developed "The Enjoyable Diet," which allows a person to eat a controlled amount of confections along with nutritious meals to accomplish your weight loss goal. The following is reprinted courtesy of the National Confectioners Association.

THE ENJOY-ABLE DIET BAL-ANCED WITH A SWEET TOUCH

The Enjoyable Diet

People eat for many reasons. Nutrition is certainly a major one, but we can't ignore the important psychological and cultural reasons which make what we eat a learned, emotional behavior. Sweets, especially confections, make us feel satisfied; they often serve as a personal "reward" (a habit learned in childhood!). Most reducing diets eliminate sweet foods and consequently fail because we are not comfortable with the meal plans and feel deprived.

The Enjoyable Diet seeks to help you reduce weight, without giving up sweets. It is scientifically UNTRUE that you must avoid confections to lose pounds. The Enjoyable Diet is a well-balanced, nutritious meal plan developed by a registered dietitian. There is nothing nutritionally wrong with including confections in a weight loss program, providing they do not replace other necessary foods. The Enjoyable Diet menus have been designed to include the recommended number of servings from the USDA's Daily Food Guide:

Servings: 4
Food Group: Vegetable & Fruit Group
Food Example: (Fresh, frozen and canned fruits, vegetables and juices)

Servings: 4
Food Group: Bread & Cereal Group
Food Example: (Breads, muffins, crackers, grains, pasta, cereal)

Servings: 2
Food Group: Milk & Cheese Group
Food Example: (Milk, yogurt, cheeses, ice cream)

Servings: 2
Food Group: Meat, Poultry, Fish & Protein Group
Food Example: (Beef, chicken, fish fillets, cheese)

Food Group: Sweets, Fat & Alcohol

Food from the Sweets, Fats & Alcohol Group should be eaten only after foods from the other four more nutritious groups have been planned for.

Food Example: (Confections, butter, margarine, cream. Alcohol is not permitted on this diet)

The daily eating pattern which follows remains the same every day, and insures that you will eat the suggested amounts from the five groups each day. Foods in the same group contain similar nutrients and in specified amounts, the same number of calories. (So, you do not have to count calories.)

You must eat **all** the food in each meal that you select. Less is NOT better, because you may not get enough nutrients to meet the minimum requirements.

This food pattern allows for one serving of confection(s) each day, which may be eaten as a snack, dessert, or anytime you want a treat. Candy is a convenient energy booster for dieters—portable, packable and portion-controlled.

Daily Eating Pattern

Breakfast

1 serving Milk & Cheese Group
1 serving Bread & Cereal Group
1 serving Vegetable & Fruit Group
1 serving Fat

Lunch

1 serving Milk & Cheese Group
2 servings Bread & Cereal Group
1 serving Meat, Poultry, Fish & Protein
   Group
1 serving Vegetable & Fruit Group
1 serving Fat

Dinner

1 serving Bread & Cereal Group
1 serving Meat, Poultry, Fish & Protein
   Group
2 servings Vegetable & Fruit Group
1 serving Fat

Bonus

1 serving of confections per day to
   be eaten anytime.

How can you have your sweets and lose weight too? "Portion Control" is the answer. The Enjoyable Diet provides 1,200 calories per day, approximately 1,000 from food in the first four food groups and 200 from confections. Remember: you must watch portion size, which determines how many calories are consumed. Serving sizes are listed in the sample meals from which you will be selecting. Follow them exactly.

Each day you may select up to 200 calories worth of confections. A chart is given listing the number of calories found in most popular varieties. If you're surprised to discover some confections contain fewer calories than you thought, you're not alone! In an informal survey, most people (women, especially) estimated that each piece of candy had more calories than it actually did. So, refer to the chart for your daily 200 calories worth of confections.

A week of breakfast, lunch, and dinner menus is provided below. Select one menu from each meal column. The meals contain simple, nutritious foods that fit today's lifestyles. Some are totable for those on-the-run, others are more suitable for at home eating. There are old favorites on the menu and a few new food ideas for adventuresome eating.

If you find a breakfast or lunch which you particularly enjoy, you may repeat it during the week. You can also choose a dinner menu for lunchtime but then you must select a lunch menu for your evening meal. You may **not** have two dinners or two lunches in one day.

Coffee, tea, or diet soda may be consumed at any time. Margarine may be substituted for butter when applicable. Servings are based on after-cooking portions.

As in most 1,200 calorie diets, to ensure that you are meeting all of your body's nutritional needs, it is recommended that a vitamin-mineral supplement with iron and zinc be taken daily. To further increase your nutritional intake, choose fortified milk, cereal and grain products, which are readily available at supermarkets—just read the label! Also, it is wise to consult with your physician before embarking on any restricted food plan.

Breakfast (Meal 1)

1 ½ toasted English muffin spread with 1 teaspoon margarine, ¼ cantaloupe and 1 cup skim milk.

2 ¾ cup bran flakes (or other unsweetened cereal) topped with 10 fresh strawberries (4 ounces orange juice may be substituted) and 1 cup low-fat (2%) milk.

3 1 slice whole wheat toast spread with ½ teaspoon margarine, broiled grapefruit half sprinkled with brown sugar, and 1 cup skim milk.

4 **Breakfast Energy Shake:**
Blend 1 cup low-fat milk (2%), ½ cup orange or grapefruit juice, 1 ice cube and vanilla extract to taste. Serve with 4 slices melba toast.

5 Citrus compote of ½ orange and ¼ grapefruit sectioned. 1 cup skim milk, ½ toasted bagel spread with 1 teaspoon margarine.

6 ½ cup hot unsweetened cereal, ½ cup papaya or mango or 6 ounces grapefruit juice, and 1 cup low-fat milk (2% fat).

7 **Sizzling Fruit:**
Roll ½ banana, cut into chunks, in 2 tablespoons wheat germ. Sauté in 1 teaspoon butter. Serve with 1 cup skim milk.

Lunch (Meal 2)

1 **Pocket Sandwich:**
1 flour tortilla filled with shredded lettuce, diced onion, 2 slices tomato, 2 ounces feta cheese, and 1 ounce chick peas. Sprinkle with 1 tablespoon diet Italian dressing.

2 **Pizza:**
Spread 2 English muffin halves with 2 tablespoons tomato sauce. Sprinkle with grated onion, green pepper, and oregano. Top with 2 ounces shredded mozzarella cheese. Broil until bubbly. Serve with cucumber and carrot sticks.

3 **Turkey Sandwich:**
Place 2 ounces cooked turkey (without skin), lettuce and 2 slices tomato between 2 slices of pumpernickel bread, spread with 1 tablespoon plain yogurt. Serve with ½ cup cole slaw.

4 **Hot Platter:**
4 ounces broiled fish fillet, garnished with lemon wedge. Serve with 1 small baked potato, topped with 1 teaspoon butter and fresh parsley, also, 1 broiled tomato sprinkled with Parmesan cheese.

5 **Tuna Salad Sandwich:**
Tuna salad (made from 2 ounces water-packed tuna, 1 teaspoon mayonnaise, chopped celery) on hard roll with lettuce, bean sprouts and/or scallions. Serve with a dill pickle.

6 **Health Salad:**
Slice and toss together ½ cucumber, ½ tomato, ½ green pepper, ¼ onion, 1 medium carrot, 3 celery stalks, ¼ cup diet Italian dressing, and ½ cup creamed cottage cheese. Place on large bed of spinach leaves topped with ¼ cup croutons. Serve with 3 bread sticks.

7 One, 8-ounce carton of low-fat lemon, vanilla or coffee flavored yogurt sprinkled with 1 teaspoon wheat germ. Serve with a bran muffin and carrot or celery sticks.

In addition, choose one fruit serving from this list to eat with each lunch (except lunch #6):
  1 medium apple, orange, peach, pear
  2 apricots
  2 plums
  2 medium prunes
  ½ banana, grapefruit or mango
  1 cup watermelon, honeydew or cantaloupe
  ½ cup fresh orange or grapefruit sections, water-packed, fruit cocktail, applesauce (unsweetened), strawberries, pineapple chunks (fresh or juice packed)

Dinner (Meal 3)

1 3 ounces broiled liver, served with 1 slice rye toast spread with 1 teaspoon butter; ½ cup asparagus; ½ cup citrus sections; and 8 ounces skim milk.

2 Beef Shish-Kabob:
2 ounces lean beef cubes, 1 onion, 1 tomato and ½ green pepper. Serve on bed of rice (½ cup) with small tossed salad, 1 tablespoon oil and vinegar dressing. Serve with a small baked apple, sprinkled with cinnamon, and 8 ounces skim milk.

3 3 ounces broiled lean veal slices. Serve with ½ cup noodles topped with 1 teaspoon butter and fresh parsley; ½ cup broccoli flavored with lemon juice; and ½ cup vanilla ice milk with ½ sliced banana.

4 4 ounces poached scallops; 2 new potatoes topped with 1 teaspoon butter; ½ cup beets; ¼ cantaloupe or honeydew melon with lime wedge and 8 ounces skim milk.

5 2 ounces lean sliced beef or hamburger patty; 1 small baked potato topped with 1 teaspoon butter; and ½ cup cooked spinach. Serve with fresh fruit parfait or ½ cup plain yogurt and ½ cup blueberries.

6 4 ounces broiled fillet of sole basted in 2 tablespoons white wine served with: 1 sliced carrot, ½ cup yellow and green squash and 1 tablespoon scallions. Also include a small spinach-mushroom salad tossed in 1 tablespoon diet Italian dressing, 1 small roll and 1 teaspoon butter. For dessert a Peach Frappe: blend 8 ounces skim milk, 1 small fresh peach, and 2 ice cubes until frothy.

7 Chicken Marengo:
3 ounces chicken (without skin) poached in small amount of water flavored with 1 cup mashed tomatoes, ½ cup diced onion, and 2 large sliced mushrooms. Serve over ½ cup noodles. Also include small lettuce salad with 1 tablespoon diet Italian dressing, 1 small pear, and 8 ounces skim milk.

All meat portions represent cooked amounts.

Choose up to 200 calories worth of confection(s) daily:

Candy	Amount	Cal.
Milk Chocolate	1.05 ounce bar	160
	.25 ounce	40
Milk Chocolate with Nuts	1.05 ounce bar	160
	.25 ounce	40
Milk Chocolate with Caramel, Nuts, and Nougat	1.5 ounce bar	210
Mini Milk Chocolate Bar with Crisp Rice	.35 ounce	52
Chocolate Covered	2.05 ounce	250
	.64 ounce	80
Chocolate Bar with Nuts and Raisins	1 ounce	142
Chocolate Bar with Pecans and Cashews	1 ounce	148

Food	Serving	Calories
Chocolate Covered Fudge Bar with Nuts and Caramels	1 ounce	139
Chocolate Coated Raisins	1 ounce (30 pieces)	120
Non-Pareils	1 ounce	132
Marshmallow	1 piece	23
Peanut Brittle	1 ounce	119
Caramel Sucker (large)	1 piece	121
Lollipop	1 piece (.9 ounces)	99
	1 piece (.6 ounces)	69
Lollipop with Chocolate Center	.49 ounce	55
Malted Milk Balls	1 piece	9
Chocolate Covered Cherries	1 piece	66
Licorice Twist	1 piece	27
Roll Mints	1 piece	7
Caramel Cube	1 piece	29
Chocolate Covered Nougat	1½ ounce bar	179
Jellies	1 ounce	92
Fruit Slice	1 piece	29
Sour Ball	1 piece	28
Mint Sandwich Parfait	1 piece	31
Peppermint Patty	1 piece	30
Candy Coated Chocolate Pieces	1 ounce	140
Candy Coated Chocolate Pieces with Peanuts	1 ounce	144
Peanut Butter Cup	1 piece	92
Spearmint Leaf	1 piece	32
Salt Water Taffy	1 piece	31
Turkish Taffy	1 ounce bar	108
Almond Bridge Mix	1 ounce (7 pieces)	154
Chocolate Covered Creams (1 pound box, 44 pieces)	1 piece	47
Chocolate Covered Creams (1 pound box, 70 pieces)	1 piece	27
Jelly Beans	1 ounce	104
Gumdrops	1 ounce (10 pieces)	98
Candy Corn	1 ounce (9 pieces)	45
Candy Cane	7 inches	110

Any discussion of weight control would not be complete without mentioning the importance of physical activity. Increasing exercise not only helps you to lose weight faster by burning more calories, it also strengthens muscle tone and encourages a general feeling of well-being. Many studies show that there is a direct rela- tionship between those who do not regularly participate in some form of physical activitiy and those who are overweight.

Here is a handy guide for measuring how many calories you burn while doing various activities:

Activity	Calories Burned Per Pound Body Weight Per Hour*
Sedentary (Sitting, Studying)	.5
Light to Moderate Exercise (Standing to Slow Walking)	.6 – 1.1
Active Exercise (Fast Walking)	1.7
Strenuous Exercise (Jogging, Running)	2.4

*Alfin-Slater, R. and Aftergood, L.: *Nutrition for Today*, Dubuque, Brown: 1973.

III

More Candyland Histories

And Now a Word From Minnie

In the 1920s, women were not expected to dine in public unescorted, as restaurants were for men and served liquor. Candy stores, however, were acceptable places for ladies. That's when George DeMet got into the act.

DeMet, who had been born in Greece in 1891, helped his brother Nicholas run his candy store in Minneapolis, Minnesota, in 1910. (The store had opened in 1892.) When the store burned, the two went to Chicago to help operate four Johnson Candy Stores started by a cousin, C. N. Johnson. Later the name was changed to DeMet's, Inc., and by the 1920s there were twelve stores in the Chicago chain.

Sandwiches were served in the candy shops in about 1916. They caught on, and the DeMet's sandwich menu quickly became a staple. It remained much the same throughout company history. In the early 1920s, soda fountains were installed.

Minnie Ohler was on duty as the candy dipper in one of the DeMet's stores in 1923 when a candy salesman came to call. The salesman showed her a new kind of candy consisting of pecans and caramel dipped in chocolate. When Minnie saw the first piece of that candy she

said, "Why, that looks like a turtle!" And, without further ado, the name "Turtle" was born. DeMet's Turtles became a household word throughout much of America. DeMet's owned the name for several decades, but eventually sold it to a Canadian-owned firm, Rowntree Demet's, Inc., which has a U.S. office in Chicago, Illinois.

George DeMet and a brother continued in the restaurant business under the name George DeMet, Inc. Their last restaurant was sold in 1977. DeMet died in 1983, but he left his mark in several ways. For one, he was most effective in advancing women's rights in terms of dining out in the 1920s. He also pounced upon the name that Minnie Ohler supplied to market a product that soon became one of America's most recognized candies, Turtles.

Cars and Railroad Engineers

Remember the golden age of American cars in the 1930s? Among the prestige makes at the time were Cadillac, Duesenberg, La Salle, Lincoln, Marmon, Packard, Peerless, Stutz, Pierce-Arrow, and the Springfield Rolls-Royce. Now which of those cars had a candy bar named after it? If you guessed Pierce-Arrow, you were on target.

The Pierce-Arrow Company, started in the 1920s, made its classic cars until 1938. The Pierces of the 1930s were superb road machines and are recognized today as star examples of the best in American automobile engineering.

In the 1930s, the Chase Candy Company (today the Chase and Poe Candy Company) of St. Joseph, Missouri, issued a Pierce Arrow candy bar that sold well for a while, but then unfortunately went the way of its namesake.

Also during the 1930s, Chase made several other candy bars that, for the most part, lived only during that decade. They were Candy Dogs, 'Tween Meals, and Casey Jones. Casey Jones?

John Luther Jones was known throughout his life as "Casey," nicknamed for his home town of Cayce, Kentucky, where he was born in 1864. In 1890, he became an engineer on the Illinois Central railroad. And on April 29, 1900, he made his last trip on the Cannonball Express.

According to the widely accepted story, he pulled into Memphis, Tennessee, and learned that the engineer scheduled for the return run was sick. Casey volunteered to take over. After getting a late start, he highballed the Cannonball Express down the track to make up for lost time.

Near Vaughan, Mississippi, he spied a freight train stopped ahead on the tracks. Unfortunately, it was too late to stop the

Cannonball, so he hollered to his fireman, "Jump, Sim, and save yourself!" Casey remained on board and rode the engine into the collision. When his body was found near the wreckage, Casey still had one hand on the brake, the other on the whistle cord.

Casey's name was immortalized in a ballad written by a friend and fellow railroad worker, Wallace Saunders. Through the ballad of "Casey Jones," Casey's deed soon made him a hero to railroad men and also to the general public. In 1938, a bronze tablet to Casey's memory was dedicated in Cayce, his home town.

In the late 1930s, the Chase Candy Company also immortalized Casey's name on a candy bar. Unfortunately, the Casey Jones candy bar, named for a railroad engineer, went the way of the candy bar named for the Pierce-Arrow. The two bars and their namesakes truly were tops in their times, but not beyond.

Chunky Square

Were you at the New York World's Fair in 1964–1965? If you were, chances are you visited Chunky Square, the Chunky Candy pavilion. It featured a completely automated candy factory that daily produced thousands of Old Nick candy bars. (Old Nick was first made by Schutter's.)

A guidebook to the fair stated, "Inside the glass-walled plant, candy centers travel in military precision along a conveyor system, become enrobed in a flowing cascade of chocolate, glide through the world's first outdoor candy cooling tunnel, and are wrapped and packaged for delivery to supermarkets."

The fair passed into oblivion, as did Chunky Square and the Old Nick candy bar. But Chunky products are still being made.

Philip Silvershein, the original manufacturer of Chunky candy bars, passed away in 1982. In addition to coming up with the Chunky bar, Silvershein created numerous candy inventions to delight his

OUT TO MUNCH

Busy coeds, like busy people everywhere, know the refreshing joy of taking time out to munch delicious OLD NICK Candy Bars...that taste-tempting blend of creamy fudge, luscious caramel, and fresh toasted nuts, covered with a thick coating of richest milk chocolate.

You'll also like BIT-O-HONEY

grandchildren. For example, for the fifth birthday of one grandchild, he presented her with a doll-sized house made entirely out of miniature Chunkies known as Cuties.

When Silvershein lived in Kew Gardens, New York, his home was mobbed every Halloween, because all the neighborhood kids knew exactly where to go for a special treat!

Chocolate and the Eighteenth Amendment

It wasn't long after World War I that the Eighteenth Amendment (prohibiting alcohol) was ratified. Federal agents (remember Eliot Ness in "The Untouchables" on TV?) tried to enforce it, but moonshiners and bootleggers kept the public well supplied. Speakeasies were the places to go for action. Customers rang the bell or rapped twice on the door. The peephole opened, and if the customer had the right card or password, he got in.

In Chicago, Al Capone and his mob kept the speakeasies well supplied with bootleg liquor. Big Al rode around in an armored car and had an army of hundreds of hoods to keep Chicago safe from other bootleggers attempting to crash the scene. Big Al also had Placido Giacobbo as an aide. During his years with Capone, Giacobbo was known as Charley, Big Al's chauffeur. It was rumored, but never substantiated, that both Charley and Big Al had a fondness for chocolate.

It was in the early thirties when an entrepreneur at the Marvel Candy Company in Chicago came up with a chocolate-covered candy bar with a rum-flavored center. It was appropriately called the 18th Amendment Bar "with that Pre-War Flavor." A jug of rum was pictured on the wrapper.

Courtesy Alan Bitterman

The bar's life in the marketplace was limited, because the Eighteenth Amendment was repealed in December, 1933. Rumor had it that the bar wasn't long for the world anyway, because both Big Al and Charley disliked it. The chocolate was okay, but the rum used in the center wasn't one of Big Al's brands.

Bluebirds and White Cliffs

You're an old-timer if you remember World War II songs such as "The White Cliffs of Dover," "Praise the Lord and Pass the Ammunition," "When the Lights Go On Again," "Don't Sit Under the Apple Tree," "There's a Star-Spangled Banner Waving Somewhere," "Comin' In on a Wing and a Prayer," Spike Jones's "Der Fuehrer's Face," and "Just Remember Pearl Harbor."

And if you were listening to the radio on Sunday, December 7, 1941, you suddenly found out where Pearl Harbor was. On December 8, you heard President Franklin Roosevelt address Congress and say, among other things, that December 7 was "a date that will live in infamy."

The Senate voted unanimously for a declaration of war on Japan. The House voted 388 to 1 for war. The lone negative vote was cast by Congresswoman Jeanette Rankin, who had also voted against the declaration of war in 1917.

The American people, caught up in a wave of patriotism that lasted through the World War II years, went all out to support the war effort. Young men and women served their country in the various branches of the military. The folks on the home front helped the war effort by working in defense industries, planting victory gardens, or just keeping the home fires burning.

The confectionery businesses contributed to morale during those dark days by helping sweeten people's lives. Many new candy bars appeared on the scene, and some of them had names that related to the military effort.

From the Walter H. Baker Company of

Dorchester, Massachusetts, came the Flying Fortress Bar. It was the civilian version of a ration bar that Baker's prepared for the U. S. Army. The Flying Fortress bar was perhaps the only Baker bar product that didn't include a picture of La Belle Chocolatier, the famous trademark of the Baker Company. Instead, on the front of the wrapper appeared a view of the B-17, one of the premier Army Air Force bombers. On the back of the wrapper, a spotter's view of the Boeing aircraft as seen from the ground was featured.

On the ground, the motor vehicle that came into the limelight during the war was the small, durable, four-wheel-drive, all-purpose Jeep. It was utilized by the armed forces throughout the world and was immortalized by the Washburn Candy Corporation of Brockton, Massachusetts, in a candy bar called Jeep.

The Charms Company of Bloomfield, New Jersey, manufactured candy bars in the early 1940s. One of those bars was Chevron. On the wrapper were reproduced the stripes indicating military rank such as corporal, sergeant, and private first class.

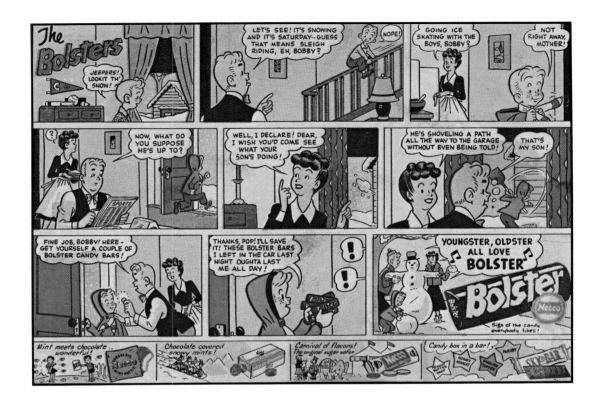

He Knows His Baby Ruth

It just hits the spot, and it's such a big piece of good candy for only a nickel.

Gee, it's good! Fresh, pure chocolate, just chock-full of toasted nuts, with a creamy center of fudge and chewy caramel that melts in your mouth.

Doesn't it make you hungry to think of it?

BABY RUTH is good for you, too, because it is made of the good things that build up your strength and muscle. That's why BABY RUTH is the American boy's favorite candy.

CURTISS CANDY COMPANY, CHICAGO

NEW YORK

BOSTON

Otto Y. Schnering, PRESIDENT

Candy Makers to the American Nation

LOS ANGELES

SAN FRANCISCO

Baby Ruth sold at the shelter house

CURTISS **Baby Ruth** America's Favorite 5¢

5¢

EIGHT Delicious Chocolates in One!

Oh Henry! is not the usual candy bar . . . . . but *eight* delicious chocolates in one, to be sliced as you need them. A "special occasion" quality in everyday size! And no $1.25 chocolates are finer in quality, or made with more infinite care.

When you slice into a bar . . . . . slice through that mellowest of milk chocolates, tender, crunchy nuts, golden, old-fashion butter cream and luscious, lingering caramel . . . . . the milky fragrance of the chocolate, the way the candy cuts, its creamier consistency, its richer and more tempting color all unite to say that this is truly a fine candy.

The *bar* form of Oh Henry! is simply a convenience for people who like

good candy during the day. A convenience, also, for hostesses who may always have a few bars in the pantry, and at a minute's notice have fine candy for teas, bridge games, after dinner and other occasions simply by slicing one, two or as many bars as are desired.

Serve Oh Henry! sliced at any time to anyone. Millions know . . . . . *and love it!*

Now made in Canada by Walter M. Lowney Co., Limited, Montreal

Write for FREE Copy of the new Oh Henry! recipe book: 60 delicious ways to serve Oh Henry!

In less than two months women mailed us over 8,000 recipes for the use of Oh Henry! in cakes, icings, puddings, ice cream, baked apples, and innumerable other desserts. Under the direction of one of the leading home economists, Mrs. Lily Haxworth Wallace, the best of these have been made into this unusual recipe book. Write for it. . . . . FREE.

WILLIAMSON CANDY COMPANY • • Chicago, Illinois

Big Chief
of the Nickel Tribe

Three-flavored bargain* from Mars' sunlit kitchens — the best-liked chocolate-
covered candy bar in all the world . . .

Milky Way 5¢ *{ 1. *Honest-to-Goodness* MILK CHOCOLATE *—from the finest imported chocolate beans* 2. GOLDEN CARAMEL 3. CREAMY CHOCOLATE MALTED MILK NOUGAT

There was no stripe for a buck private, but there was a Buck-Private candy bar. It was made and sold in the East by Henry Heide, Inc., of New York City. The same bar was manufactured and sold in the West by another company.

The Fort Worth Candy Company in Texas issued the Commando bar. A commando was a member of a small fighting force that was specially trained for making quick, destructive raids against enemy-held areas.

The Shotwell Manufacturing Company of Chicago put out its Big Yank bar. For the most part, the term "Yank" was an affectionate one, applied to American servicemen the world over.

The Deran Confectionery Company, of Cambridge, Massachusetts, picked up a name for a candy bar that symbolized *the* place to go for refreshments on a military base—the Post Exchange, or PX. Deran did the Army one better by adding the name of a meal to come up with their bar name of P-X Lunch.

World War II is now a memory. But for those who can remember, Flying Fortress, Jeep, Chevron, Buck Private, Commando, Big Yank, and P-X Lunch conjure up a time when all America was united, albeit in war. Those candy bars were indeed signs of the times.

Tale of Two Cities

Two cities that have captured the heart of America are San Francisco and Miami. In 1935, Joe Burke composed the music and Edgar Leslie wrote the lyrics for a song that became a pop classic, "Moon Over Miami." As far as that city by the bay goes, who can forget Tony Bennett's "I Left My Heart in San Francisco," written in 1962 by George Cory with lyrics by Douglas Cross.

In 1936, the movie *San Francisco*, starring Clark Gable, Jeanette MacDonald, and Spencer Tracy, reached the screen. Special effects in that film included a mindboggling earthquake sequence. A movie on the lighter side, *Hello Frisco, Hello*, appeared in 1943 and starred Alice Faye. At one point, Faye was a singer with Rudy Vallee's band. A candy bar named after Rudy appeared briefly in the early 1930s.

Suffice it to say, the candy industry also did its part to bring the names of these two cities to the public on candy bar wrappers. In the early 1930s, a Miami Bar wrapper appeared, but no manufacturer's name was printed on it. And some time in the 1940s, the D. L. Clark Company came out with their Miami bar.

In the late 1920s or early 1930s, the Pangburn Company of Fort Worth, Texas, manufactured a Frisco Bar. And in the 1940s, Mars, Inc., of Chicago produced a Frisco bar that sold for ten cents.

Both Miami and San Francisco are still going strong. But the four candy bars that bore their names are no longer on the scene. Instead, they rest peacefully in the places set aside for them in Candyland Cemetery.

For He's a Jolly Good Feller

From the late 1930s to the early 1950s, major league baseball had an impressive group of pitchers. Perhaps the premier performer of those hurlers was Bob Feller of the Cleveland Indians. He had a zinger of a fastball, a wicked curve, and just enough wildness to keep batters loose at the plate.

In the 1940s, Feller came into his own. His career started in 1936 and ended in 1956. Among his many accomplishments were leading the American League in strikeouts seven times and wins six times, and pitching three no-hitters. Had he not served in the Navy for four years during World War II, Feller would most certainly have added even more glories to his record. He was elected to the Baseball Hall of Fame in 1962.

From the late 1930s to the early 1940s, a Bob Feller candy bar was in the marketplace. The bar was similar to the Baby Ruth and Love Nest chocolate-covered nut rolls. The Euclid Candy Company of

Brooklyn was the manufacturer. Cy Slapnicka, then general manager of the Indians and Feller's friend, negotiated the contract arrangements with the candy company, and Feller received royalties on sales.

Courtesy Barry Halper

The Bob Feller bar was a moderately successful seller, but World War II caused the bar's demise. During its career, the Bob Feller bar was top drawer, just as was Bob Feller the pitcher.

Of Cabbages and Kings and Sauerkraut

The technique for making sauerkraut really hasn't changed since it was first recorded by the early Romans, who acquired it from the Orient. Salt was added to shredded cabbage, then the cabbage was allowed to ferment.

Sauerkraut making was forgotten by Europeans until the conquering hordes of tatars reintroduced it to Austria in the thirteenth century, bringing it in from China. The Austrians gave sauerkraut its name (literally, "sour cabbage"). It was passed along to neighbors, and the Germans especially welcomed it.

In the days of the sailing ships, perhaps the greatest danger on long sea voyages was from scurvy. The great English explorer, Captain James Cook, believed scurvy had something to do with a sailor's diet. When he discovered that the Germans rarely had scurvy and always had barrels of sauerkraut with them on voyages, Cook decided to make use of sauerkraut in 1772 aboard his ship, the *Resolution*, on a trip to the South Pacific.

Captain Cook was a smart cookie. He realized his English sailors would never voluntarily eat this German food, no matter how good it was for them, unless they were tricked into doing so. What did Cook do? He had barrels of sauerkraut put on deck. Signs above each of the barrels read, "For Officers' Use Only!"

Cook's trickery worked. Sailors were never seen taking sauerkraut, but the barrels' contents diminished day by day. Most important, the sauerkraut provided needed dietary elements, and no scurvy was reported aboard the *Resolution* on that voyage.

Sauerkraut is sour and candy is sweet, but there were and are candy bars that made use of the sauerkraut name for confectionery products. In the late 1920s and 1930s, the Sour Krout Candy Company of Chicago made their Sour Krout bar. A Sauerkraut Bar was manufactured in 1949 by the Bayou Candy Company of New Orleans, later a division of the Pangburn Candy Company. The bar was made from freshly shredded coconut, which looked like cabbage shredded to make sauerkraut. Soon, however, the "sauer" was dropped and the name was changed to Long Boy Kraut, which was trademarked. (The Bayou Division was purchased from Pangburn a few years ago by the American Candy Manufacturing Company of Selma, Alabama.)

LONG BOY "COCONUT"

Delicious Coconut Caramel Candy Bars

Sometime after the Civil War, the Gillman Candy Company opened in Selma. Emille Gillman was a German immigrant who had been a baker for the Confederate Army during the War Between the States. In those days, bakers and confectioners were usually one and the same. In 1899, Gillman sold his business to Joe and Ming Wilkins and M. M. Lehman, who renamed it the American Candy Company. American Candy is now a large manufacturer of candy and markets its products in all fifty states. It has a hard-candy license for Disney.

In the 1930s, American Candy made a number of candy bars—Mammoth Peanut Bar, Mogul Peanut Bar, Peco Flake Bar, and Coconut Cream Bar. The bars were phased out in the 1950s, so the only bar presently made by American Candy is the Long Boy at the Bayou Division in New Orleans.

Individually wrapped pieces

Mrs. E. V. Dicks worked for American Candy from 1931 until 1974. After her retirement, she wrote a paper titled "My Recollections." Here are some of her memories of the good old days:

In 1931 when I started working for the candy factory. . . Mr. Lehman was president and acted as sales manager. I started as stenographer, more or less for Mr. Lehman and wrote his personal letters, ordered his cigars, and arranged his bridge parties. Must admit I was always slightly afraid of him. He often drenched me with cough syrup that contained cod liver oil when I had a cold, and even sent me home at times.

He was a shrewd businessman and an excellent salesman. He often traveled to New York via train to solicit business from the 5¢ and 10¢ stores, securing orders by giving the buyers a quart or so of moonshine whiskey.

The office, shipping room, and a storage room was on the first floor. Candy was manufactured on the second floor. Corn syrup which came in wood barrels or steel drums, and sugar which came in cloth or paper sacks was stored in the basement. The boiler room and a storage place for boxes and cartons was on the ground floor adjacent to the shipping room.

In the early years of my employment, all office work was done by hand and our office equipment was limited to two manual typewriters and an adding machine. The adding machine sat on a tall iron frame. One stood to add and operated the machine with a hand lever on the side.

A large iron coal heater that sat in the

middle of the floor warmed the place, and two ceiling fans served as air conditioners. Large windows that opened out also helped cool the office. A shelf in the shipping room held our large cooler of ice water; also a bucket of water with a dipper, and a wash basin as there was no wash room.

Sawdust and shavings were used to fire the boiler. The sawdust pile also served as a hiding place for a sack of sugar whenever the fireman felt the need of a sack for his friend in the moonshine business.

Sugar and corn syrup was taken up by a hand-operated elevator from the basement to the second floor kitchen. The candy was cooked in open kettles and pulled on pulling machines, then finished by hand. There were men who worked as candy spinners, rollers, and strippers. Women did most of the wrapping and packing of the candy. These people were paid by the number of batches of candy that they made or the number of packages wrapped and cases packed. No certain number of hours were worked.

One employee...known as The Big Stick Candy Man...made large sticks of candy. As he worked he drank about a quart of fruit juice between batches of candy. The largest stick he produced weighed 65 pounds and was used in decorating the window of S. H. Kress & Co. one Christmas.

The payroll was figured by hand and workers paid in cash. Office help was paid weekly by check. My first salary was $9.00 a week (1931). Later $12.50, then $15.00. The $15.00 per week made me feel rich.

What a wonderful memento Mrs. Dick has left us about the candy business in olden days. They were indeed rich—at least in memories, if not in salary.

George Vancouver and the Mountains

In the late eighteenth century, Captain George Vancouver roamed the Pacific Northwest charting names for the physical features in the landscape he encountered. It was Vancouver who, in 1792, from the mouth of the Columbia River, saw the mountain that he named Mount St. Helens. He named the mountain "in honor of His Britannic Majesty's Ambassador at the Court of Madrid...." The ambassador had been raised to the Irish peerage as Baron St. Helens.

In the journal of the Lewis and Clark expedition, on October 19, 1805, Captain Clark noted the sighting of "Mount St. Helens, laid down by Vancouver as visible from the mouth of the Columbia...."

Captain Vancouver was also responsible for the name of the highest mountain in what is now the state of Washington. He named the peak Mount Rainier in honor of Rear Admiral Peter Rainier of the British Navy. But in 1853, Theodore Winthrop one-upped Vancouver. He declared the name to be Tacoma after a generic Indian word for snow-covered mountains.

Later, a city developed on Commencement Bay with the name of Tacoma. That city grew and eventually debated whether to officially change the name of Mount Rainier to Mount Tacoma. The spirited name controversy continued throughout the state for many years.

What has all of this to do with candy? Well, in 1907, Harry Brown, who had earlier worked in the retail candy business, started a candymaking business in Tacoma that he named Oriole Candies. A popular slogan developed by Oriole was "Best in the West." One of Brown's competitors was Frank Mars, who worked in Tacoma in 1911. Mars wasn't successful in Tacoma and eventually moved to Minneapolis.

J. C. Haley soon joined Harry Brown in the candy business to form Brown and Haley. Just before World War I, their Mountain Bar was introduced. When this bar first appeared, it was called the Mt. Tacoma. There was an intense rivalry between the citizens of Tacoma and Seattle as to whether or not Mount Rainier's name should be officially changed. Tacomans passionately referred to the peak as Mt. Tacoma.

In time it became apparent to the candy company managers that, if they wished to increase the sales of their candy bar in Seattle, they would have to change its name. So around 1925, the name was changed to Mountain® Bar. Mountain Bar ranks as one of the early candy bars that is still in production. It's now marketed in about eighteen Western states. The original bar had a vanilla cream center. In later years, Cherry Mountain and Peanut Butter Mountain bars joined the production line (and don't forget Gremlins).

In the late 1920s and 1930s, some popular candy bars from Brown and Haley were Iceberg, Fun, Hello Dear, Totem Poles, Malted Milk, Black Walnut, Peanut Pattie, Snoose, Rugged, and Strawberry Shortcake. Yes, Strawberry Shortcake was a candy bar long before the name was chosen for the doll and accessories that now capture little girls' hearts.

Other bars that Brown and Haley marketed at one time were Fun Bar, Johnny Peanut Bar, Mint Cream Bar, Violet Crumbles, and Victoria Cream.

After World War I, Brown and Haley's Almond Roca Buttercrunch appeared and quickly became their most widely distributed product (now worldwide).

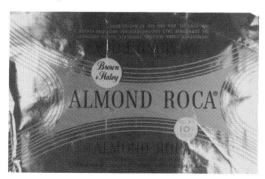

A most popular collector's item was packed with Mountain Bars. Called Smart Cards they were printed on the cardboard inserts inside the candy bar wrapper. Smart Cards numbered 1 through 97 were inserted in Mountain Bars. Cards 98 through 100 were also packed with Fun Bars and Cherry Mountain Bars.

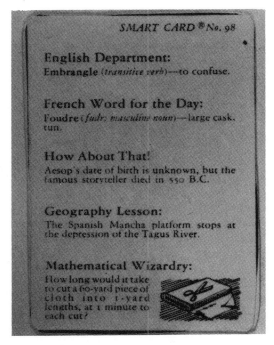

Each card carried a variety of educational trivia on the front. The back presented a joke, cartoon, and the answer to a math problem posed on the other side. Smart Cards, sorry to say, are no longer around, but Mountain Bar varieties are, along with Almond Roca.

On boxes of the three versions of Mountain Bars is the slogan, "Brown & Haley makes 'em Daily, 'cept Sunday."

Bows and Arrows and Breweries

When Indians began raiding his brewery, John Schuler began to wonder whether the beer business was a good one to be in. John had immigrated from Germany in the early 1850s and had founded his Castle Rock Brewery in 1854 along the Mississippi River in southern Wisconsin. In the post-Civil War days, the brewery also operated as a roadhouse and was patronized by settlers, rivermen, stagecoach travelers, and Indians. At times the Indians would whoop it up and arrows would start flying through the windows while the Schuler family huddled under the dining room table for safety.

The beer business prospered for many years. But the Schuler family eventually decided to try making their livelihood in a line other than beer. They moved across the river to Winona, Minnesota, where they started the Vienna Bakery and Schuler Ice Cream Company. In 1907, they founded the Schuler Chocolate Factory. Hand-dipped chocolates were made first. Later on other candies were added, including one of the early candy bars, Cherry Humps. Over the years, Schuler also made such bars as Mint Humps, Milk Humps, Pecan Humps, Walnut Humps, Almond Humps, and Brazil Humps.

In a 1920 Schuler price list was one five-cent candy bar, Schuler Big Stix. The other bars sold for ten cents. They were Cherry Humps, Pineapple Humps, Yum Yum Bar, Nut Nougatine, Sunny Jim, Carmanut Bar, Karmelkream Bar, Old Glory Bar, Tutti Frutti Bar, Goodenuff Bar, Good Stuff, Big Four, and Schuler's Chocolate Nougat.

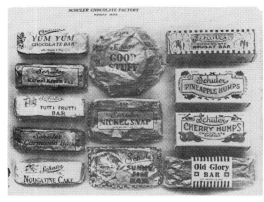

In 1923, Schuler took over the McKussick Towl Company of Minneapolis. In 1925, they purchased the Ramer Candy Company of St. Paul. Some of the candy bars manufactured under the Ramer name were Chocolate Nougat Bar, Chocolate Covered Cherries, Chocolate Peanut Bar, Maple Nut Whip, Chocolate Covered Caramallow, Dixie Nut Bar, Chocolate Walnut Bar, Ramer's Opera and Cake, Chocolate Cream, Chocolate Maple Walnut, and Chocolate Peppermints.

Schuler absorbed the Winona Candy Company in the 1920s, and acquired some of the lines of the Funke Candy Company of Boston.

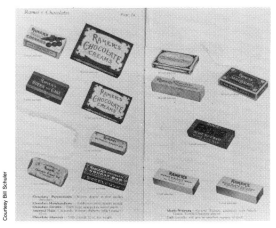

Frank Mars, who had opened his candy business in Minneapolis in 1920 after moving east from Tacoma, discontinued his business in the late 1920s before re-opening in the Chicago area. The Schuler Company manufactured the Milky Way Bar while Mars was out of operation. When Mars opened in the Chicago area he bought back the rights to the Milky Way Bar for five thousand dollars.

In the early 1920s, the Schuler Company issued a catalog that listed not only their products, but also products of other companies that Schuler handled. These included Planter's Jumbo Block, Runkel's Sweet Milk Chocolate with Fruit and Nuts, Mazarr Bar, Ambrosia's Chocolate Bark, Zatek Almond, Zatek Eatmores, and Hershey's Sweet Milk Chocolate. One of the Hershey labels in the catalog carried the interesting slogan, "More Sustaining than Meat."

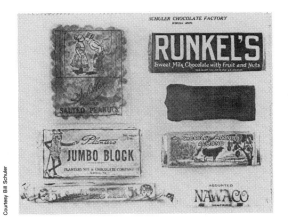

In addition to the bars listed, other Schuler bar products were included in the catalog—Nickel Snap and Nougatine Cake were two. Others were Paramount Hash, Karamel Cream Egg, Cocoanut Fudge Bar, Cocanut Log, Pecan Roll, Walnut Roll, Chocolate Covered Caramel, Milk Chocolate, and Maple Walnut Creams. A This-N bar consisted of various segments with different centers and was chocolate covered.

The Schuler Chocolate Factory fell on hard times during the Great Depression and went bankrupt in 1933. It emerged as the present Schuler Candy Company.

In the early 1960s, Schuler sold the popular ten-cent Cherry Nut bar. In 1967, Schuler bought the Sperry Candy Company from the Pearson Candy Company. The Sperry line of Easter candy, Christmas Santas, and various coconut pieces is still being produced along with the Cherry Humps bar. Some of the Sperry bars that carried the Schuler imprint in the late 1960s and early 1970s were Cold Turkey, Parfait, and Snow-Maid. Snow Cherry and Lemon Whip also carried the Schuler label.

In 1978, Schuler was purchased by Brock Candy Company of Chattanooga, Tennessee, but it continues as a separate corporation, still producing Cherry Humps, Gooney Bears, and other fine candies.

If John Schuler were around today, he'd be mighty proud of what he started. And undoubtedly he'd be a bit thankful to the Indians whose arrows steered his family in the right direction, toward Schuler Chocolates, Inc.

The Galloping Ghost

In 1983, Herschel Walker signed a pro football contract before starting his senior year at Georgia University. Before Walker's time, however, another collegian signed a pro contract. His flair for football attracted attention to his team and all of pro football. His name was Harold "Red" Grange, and he had a fabulous football record at the University of Illinois from 1923 to 1925. He became nationally known as The Galloping Ghost, or The Wheaton Iceman (he worked summers delivering blocks of ice in Wheaton, Illinois). In his best college performance in 1924, he scored five touchdowns and set up a sixth with a pass in a game against Michigan. He turned pro immediately following his last college football game.

Professional football was struggling in 1925 when entrepreneur Charles C. Pyle sold Red Grange on the idea of playing the pro game. Grange had received several offers from the Chicago Bears, but he hadn't answered them because his interest wasn't in pro ball at the time. His later talk with Pyle convinced Grange that Pyle would be a good manager for his professional career—especially when he heard such things as "How would you like to make a hundred thousand dollars . . . maybe even a million?" In the 1920s, those sums were enough to buy a good supply of candy bars.

After Grange's last college game, Pyle, George Halas of the Bears, and two other negotiators reached an agreement for hiring the "Red Grange/C.C. Pyle Company." The agreement covered the Bears' remaining league games, plus a nationwide tour of exhibition games. On Thanksgiving Day, Grange played his first game for the Bears against the Chicago Cardinals before a capacity crows of sixteen thousand. The game ended in a 0-0 tie.

The first part of the tour proved to be quite a grind, as the Bears and Grange played eight games in eight cities in only twelve days! One of those games was with the New York Giants in the Polo Grounds in New York City. About seventy-three thousand fans jammed the stands to see Grange and the Bears defeat the Giants 17 to 9. Another twenty thousand fans jockeyed for position atop Coogan's Bluff overlooking the Polo Grounds, as well as on roofs of apartment houses overlooking the stadium. The next stop on that tour was Washington, D.C., where Grange was taken to the White House and introduced to President Calvin Coolidge as "Red Grange, who plays with the Bears." To this introduction Coolidge replied, "Young man, I always liked animal acts."

The second part of the tour included eight more games, but they were spread over a month's time.

Charley Pyle decided to cash in on Grange's popularity in fields other than football. He made agreements and signed

contracts to have Grange's name affixed to such items as cigarettes, a sausage sandwich, ginger ale, a fountain pen, a doll, shoes, socks, and so forth. Grange even became a movie star.

His most famous movie was made in 1926 and was called *A Minute to Play*. As far as sports movies went, it was well above the norm and received some good reviews. In the same year, Grange decided to play in a new league and for a new team, because Pyle and the Bears' management couldn't come to a contract agreement. The new team, formed by Pyle, was called the New York Yankees and played in a new league Pyle formed as a showcase for his client. But the league folded at the end of the season, and the next year Grange was back with the Bears.

The Shotwell Manufacturing Company of Chicago signed with Pyle for the use of Grange's name on a candy bar. After the appearance of Grange's movie, a series of twenty-four scenes from the film was issued on cards packaged with the Red Grange candy bar.

One of 24 scenes from Red Grange's famous movie "One Minute To Play." Packed with SHOTWELL'S RED GRANGE Candy Bars

24

The Red Grange bar was a good seller during the height of Grange's career. But when his popularity waned, so did candy bar sales, and the Red Grange bar eventually disappeared from the marketplace.

Shotwell made many other candy bars during the 1920s and 1930s. Some of them were Strongheart, Car-Load, Sure Mike, Fig Sundae, Good Going, Molly O, Handy Andy, Cherry Cream, Chang, Caramel Sundae, Big Egg, and White Log. Good 1930s sellers were Little Orphan Annie, Fire Chief, and Roasty Toasty.

During the 1940s, Hi-Mac, Big Yank, and Shur-Mac were good sellers. Puritan marshmallows were a staple product of the company, too.

Shotwell also produced a general line of candy and was an important confectioner in terms of sales. In 1952, the Shotwell Manufacturing Company was taken over by the Chase Candy Company, which phased out the candy bars but continued to manufacture some of the marshmallow products.

Shotwell left its mark on the professional sports scene, however, as it was perhaps the first candy company to contract for the use of a sports personality's name on a candy bar. And while they were active in their fields, Grange the football player and Grange the candy bar were winners. "Cash and Carry" Pyle, as C. C. Pyle became known, didn't do too badly either!

Paul Revere Slept Here

Paul Revere was born in 1735 in Boston. He pursued the trade of silversmith and was active in patriotic causes. In fact, he was one of the leaders of the Sons of Liberty, who held the Boston Tea Party. In 1775, he and two other couriers rode from Charlestown to Lexington, alerting the countryside that the British were coming. Revere died in 1818.

In 1770, Paul Revere bought a house that had been built around 1680. Today that house is the only surviving seventeenth-century structure in Boston. Revere lived in the house with his family until 1800. During the nineteenth century, Boston's North End, where the house was located, was an overcrowded, impoverished neighborhood. The house served as a cigar factory, grocery store, a candy factory, and a tenement. In the early 1900s, the house faced demolition, but was saved for posterity by the Paul Revere Memorial Association. In 1907 it was turned into a museum.

The Paul Revere House was a candy factory in the mid-1880s, with a sign in the window that read, "Home Made Candy, Wholesale and Retail." In January 1884, the Miller Candy Company began in that building. Initially a retail confectionery, it later branched out as a wholesale jobber. Charles H. Miller started the business, and when he died three years later, two of his sons took over the retailing and Charles N. Miller took over the manufacturing and jobber business. The Charles N. Miller Company is still located in the Boston area, in Watertown, Massachusetts.

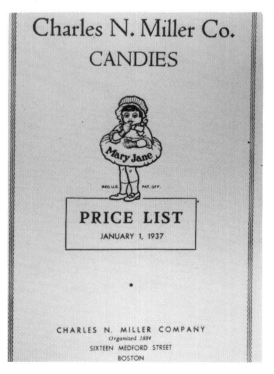

Charles N. Miller Co.
CANDIES

Mary Jane

REG. U.S.   PAT. OFF.

PRICE LIST
JANUARY 1, 1937

•

CHARLES N. MILLER COMPANY
Organized 1884
SIXTEEN MEDFORD STREET
BOSTON

FIVE CENT BARS

		Net per Box
BIG MARY JANE — *five cents each*	27 count	.60
Note the additional three pieces for the retailer. This is a new packing. The bars are wrapped in foil and cellophane.		
BIG DEARO — *five cents each*	27 count	.60
Also contains the extra three pieces for the retailer.		
OLD FASHIONED MOLASSES — *five cents each*	24 count	.60
An unusually good piece of Molasses Candy		
MARY JANES — *two for five cents*	72 count	.96
	48 count	.64
DEAROS — *two for five cents*	72 count	.96
	48 count	.64

CHOCOLATE COVERED

COCOANUT JUMBLES
Made of fresh cocoanut, deliciously toasted, and chocolate covered. Foil wrapped . . . . . 24 count .64

LIZA JANE — *one cent each*
A chocolate covered Mary Jane . . . . . . 120 count .62½

~~~~~

CONDITIONS

Full freight allowed on shipments of one hundred pounds or more.
All prices subject to change without notice.
No goods will be accepted in return unless written authorization for the return has been obtained.

CHARLES N. MILLER CO.

were three cents a pound, sugar three to three-and-a-half cents a pound, and corn syrup two-and-a-half cents."

Mary Janes, in bar form, as well as smaller sizes, and a recently introduced chocolate-covered version, are still being made today.

One of the early candies made by Miller was the Dearo, a penny candy that was a chewy chocolate with a peanut butter center. The name was borrowed from a political group that the Honorable John "Honey Fitz" Fitzgerald called his "dear ol' North Enders." Honey Fitz was a congressman and mayor who lived in the North End. The Fitzgerald home was close to the Revere House. In 1890, the Fitzgerald home was the birthplace of Rose, wife of Ambassador Joseph P. Kennedy and mother of President John F. Kennedy. The Dearo candy later became a candy bar and was called Big Dearos. Neither Dearos nor Big Dearos are being made today.

In 1914, the Mary Jane one-cent candy was introduced. Later it was sold as a five-cent candy bar. A molasses candy jacket took the place of the chocolate-flavored jacket of the Dearo. An employee of the company at the time said, "When we started making Mary Jane candy, our floor lady made $2.50 a week. Peanuts

Over the years, the Charles N. Miller Company made many candy bars that are no longer around. Some of them were Babylon, both plain and chocolate flavored; Molasses Peanut Butter Crisp; Holli-bars; Have-A-Mack; Toff-O-Luxe; Riteoff; Wampum; Dolce; Cocoanut Jumbles; Chips; and Old Fashioned Molasses. Another Boston firm, the W. A. Miller Company, also made an Old Fashioned Molasses bar in the 1940s.

In 1941, the Charles N. Miller Company handled the Rolo bar in the United States. That bar was picked up by the Hershey Company in 1971.

In a 1937 price list, the various Miller items reflected wholesale and retail costs of the times. Candy bars selling at five cents retail were sold by the box for sixty cents. The boxes contained twenty-seven bars! Also included in that price list was a chocolate-covered Mary Jane called the Liza Jane.

Had Paul Revere known what was to transpire in his house in the future, he might have modified his famous warning to say, "In addition to the British, the Dearos and the Mary Janes are coming!"

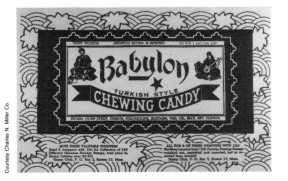

When You Need a Light, Strike a Match

There are numerous matchbook cover collectors throughout the United States. Some collectors have thousands of covers in their collection, and some of those collections include matchbook advertisements for candy items.

The matchbook industry has carried all kinds of advertising over the years. In the 1930s and 1940s, candy bar manufacturers often utilized that medium. Two of the bars advertised were Schutter's Old Nick and Schutter's Bit-O-Honey. Boyer Brothers of Altoona, Pennsylvania, advertised their MalloCup, and on the inside cover was advertised Boyer's Almond Mallo.

118

Curtiss Candy Company's Otto Schnering, who was into all forms of advertising, plugged his Baby Ruth and Butterfinger bars. In the 1930s, when quarter-pound candy bars were popular, the Curtiss Jolly Jack bar even carried the slogan, "¼ lb. 5¢," right on the matchbook cover.

When a Penny Went a Long Way

It was during the heart of the Great Depression in the early 1930s that the one-cent candy bar first appeared. All kinds of penny candy had been around for years, but the wrapped one-cent bar wasn't born until the 1930s.

Mrs. Ruth Patterson remembers the time well, as she worked for the Chicago candy company that produced the first wrapped penny bar. Here is what she had to say about those times:

Otto Schnering, head of the Curtiss Candy Company, brought relief to a great many people, many of whom literally did not know where their next meal was coming from. He introduced the penny Baby Ruth and Butterfinger bars, putting plants on around-the-clock, four-to-six hour shifts. By this short shift plan he made it possible for the maximum number of families to survive. Also he brought a little joy to the frightened people of the nation who could now occasionally find a spare penny to indulge in a treat and buy a little candy bar.

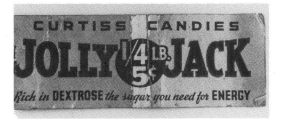

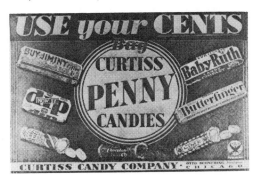

I worked on the switchboard near the entrance to Plant One, at Belmont near Halsted, where the penny Baby Ruth bars were made. (Butterfinger 1¢ bars were made at another location, North Pier Terminal.) From my vantage point at the switchboard I could see everyone who came and went.

While most of the workers were typical factory workers, a great many were people who in normal times would be working in jobs "more worthy of them"— but they all were very grateful to have any job at all which put food on the table.

The wrappers (young girls who carefully but rapidly wrapped each little bar and placed it in its box) were a happy group as they came out of the wrapping room on their breaks or at the end of their shifts. They didn't loiter though, as this was all piece work (it was before the day of the wrapping machine).

They were supervised by older women— foreladies. One of the foreladies was different. She was a gentle, motherly widow, obviously from the "right side of the tracks." She stopped by and talked with me when she had time and occasionally launched into Shakespearean quotes.

Another unusual person was the guard/doorman on one of the shifts. His father was a Scottish Presbyterian minister in Canada and his mother was a book lover who had had a book of poetry published. He had arrived in Chicago (probably by boxcar) with no money and with holes in the soles of his shoes (he had cardboard inside them). I never found out what his profession had been, but he really made his doorkeeper job an opportunity to give a lift to everyone who came near. And I don't mean with just an automatic, "Have a nice day."

Then there was the young couple with the small baby. They sometimes went hungry but were so happy that their jobs made it possible to see that their baby had everything it needed.

Mrs. Patterson's words are indicative of those times when life wasn't easy, but people learned to grin and bear it.

Otto Schnering's one-cent bars caught the public's fancy, so it was natural that other confectionery companies followed suit. Other popular one-cent bars turned out to be Oh Henry! and Chicken Dinner.

Schnering never was one to let the moss grow under his feet. He decided to go one step further now that others were in the one-cent bar business. He did it by introducing two-cent candy bars. Those bars were launched to retailers by way of a colorful brochure that pictured each of the two-cent bars at actual size. The two-cent bars weighed one-and-a-half ounces, so they were great buys.

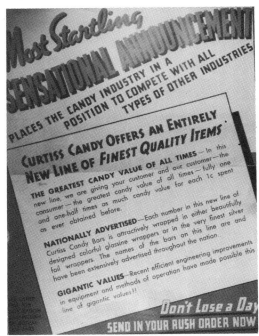

In addition to two-cent Baby Ruth and Butterfinger bars, Schnering manufactured Buy Jiminy (a peanut bar) and Kandy Kake (chocolate pudding with a chocolate covering). The Milk Nut Loaf had a marshmallow center and was covered in chocolate and topped with peanuts. Nick-aloaf was a chocolate-covered marshmallow-center bar without the peanuts. Foxxy was a nougat-center bar covered with chocolate. Curtiss Mints were chocolate-covered mint-flavored creams. All those two-cent bars had real potential marketwise, but never really got off the ground. For some reason, the buying public stuck with either one-cent or five-cent bars, but not the two-centers.

Some three-cent bars also appeared in the late 1930s. The Hollywood Candy Company made several three-cent candy bars. And the Klein Chocolate Company, Inc. of Elizabethtown, Pennsylvania, sold a popular three-cent chocolate bar, the Lunch Bar, that lasted in the marketplace for a number of years. It weighed five-sixths of an ounce and contained peanuts. Klein also made a five-cent bar that weighed a full ounce. Called Nic-L-Nut, it was the same as Lunch Bar except for the difference in weight and price.

The one-, two-, and three-cent bars, had their day in the sun, but the bars that hadn't disappeared by the 1940s were done in by World War II.

College Days

In the 1920s, flagpole sitting was the *in* thing to do. Man O' War was *the* horse. Charles Lindbergh was the pilot, Rudolph Valentino the Silent Lover, Jack Dempsey the boxer, and Clara Bow, the It Girl. (Clara was the flapper who said, "Either you have it or you don't.")

Raccoon coats and snappy hats for the gentlemen, and bobbed hair, short skirts, silk stockings, and low-cut gowns for the ladies were the fashion of the time. Attending college was fashionable, too, so confectionery people produced candy bars for the college market.

One of the first college-directed bars came out in 1922. The five-cent College Special was made by the Merrill Candy Company of Merrill, Wisconsin. Soon after, the Bradley, Smith Company, Inc., of New Haven, Connecticut, introduced a number of candy bars with the name Yale on them. Two of the Bradley, Smith bars were the Blue Boy (named after a Yale football player, Albie Booth, whose nickname was Little Boy Blue) and the Boo-La bar. (All together now, "Boo-La Boo-La, Boo-La Boo-La!")

In the late 1920s and early 1930s, the Pangburn Company of Forth Worth, Texas, produced a Co-Eds bar, a kind of peanut brittle. And not to be outdone, a company in Pittsburgh, Pennsylvania, called itself the Co-Ed Candy Company. One of their bars in the early 1930s was a one-cent Butterscotch bar.

PANGBURN COMPANY
FT. WORTH, TEX.

In California in the 1930s, the Hoffman Candy Company honored the University of Southern California by issuing the Trojan Twins (with two bars in the wrapper) and the Touch Down bar. And in Zion, Illinois, Zion Industries decided to capitalize on another aspect of college sports when it issued its Cheer Leader bar in the early 1930s.

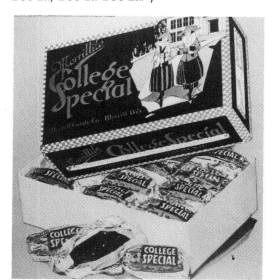

Not to be outdone, in 1931 the Sperry Candy Company of Milwaukee decided to zero in on the biggie social event of the college years—the prom. That's when the Sperry Prom Queen candy bar (two ounces or more) hit the streets.

Courtesy Alan Bitterman

Most of these bars passed into candyland oblivion by the mid-1930s, if not sooner. Candy bars with college connections were no longer in, and students were holding onto their nickels waiting for the next fad to come along. Remember when the unseemly craze of swallowing live goldfish started in 1939? That was when Lothrop Withington, Jr., swallowed a three-inch goldfish to win a ten dollar bet at Harvard Union. It wasn't long before the five-cent goldfish replaced the nickel candy bar in the college consumer market. Bars came back, however, when goldfish lost their appeal as a snack item.

What Happened When Henri and Daniel Collaborated

In the late 1800s, Henri Nestlé began intensive research on milk products and innovative applications of the condensed milk process in the small town of Vevey, Switzerland.

Meanwhile, his next-door neighbor, Daniel Peter, was attempting to combine chocolate with milk, but the results were disappointing in terms of quality and flavor.

One day Henri and Daniel were discussing their respective experiments. On a whim they decided to try mixing Nestlé's sweetened condensed milk with Peter's plain chocolate paste. The combination was prepared in one of Nestlé's machines, and then taken to Peter's plant for final processing. Voila! In 1875 milk chocolate was born.

The first Nestlé chocolate plant in America opened in the early 1900s in Fulton, New York. Now there are plants in Burlington, Wisconsin, Salinas, California, and Bloomington, Illinois.

Nestlé processes its own fresh milk daily. At Fulton, the largest Nestlé plant, about 500,000 to 600,000 pounds of milk are processed daily. The plant produces approximately one million pounds of chocolate daily when running at full capacity.

Also processed daily are about 400,000 pounds of cocoa beans. It takes approximately four hundred beans to make one pound of chocolate.

Today the Fulton plant has more than one thousand employees and sixty buildings on thirty-seven acres. Two of the employees, Harold Kenyon and Phil Williams, are organoleptic analysts. In plain language, they are called chocolate tasters. They have a combined total of sixty-three years of experience in the chocolate business. Each samples an average of one-and-a-half pounds of chocolate every day and walks an average of four to five miles throughout the plant.

Kenyon and Williams make use of their senses as they analyze the chocolate's flavor, odor, mouth-feel, appearance, and texture. When sampling, these chocolate tasters use a knife to carve off a piece of chocolate about the size of a pea, which they then roll around in their mouths to gather sensory impressions.

There is a difference in texture and "mouth feel" between the European standard for milk chocolate and the American one. Swiss chocolatiers most often refine chocolate through a lengthy process to achieve a smooth, melt-in-the-mouth chocolate. Most United States manufacturers allow for less refining time.

Soda crackers or water are available to the tasters if they wish to clear their palates before analyzing a small sample carved from a control piece of chocolate that meets the established standards. Each sample tasted must match this standard for quality control.

Phil Williams has no problem staying trim and fit. He says the job doesn't bother him a bit as far as weight goes. He gets a good bit of exercise in his daily walks throughout the plant, and, like so many people in the candy business, he has learned that chocolate should be enjoyed and savored, not gulped down in large quantity.

Harold Kenyon grew up in Fulton, and early in life he decided that someday he would work at the Nestlé plant. He admits that, as a youngster, his favorite candy bar wasn't a Nestlé, but the Beich Whiz bar, which is no longer being made.

Sure enough, Kenyon ended up at the plant, and over the years he worked his way up to become a chocolate taster. He's put on perhaps five pounds in the twenty-nine years he's worked for Nestlé. Kenyon says those extra few pounds came not from the factory, but from his wife's homemade chocolate chip cookies. He finds them a great snack after a busy day at the factory.

Both Kenyon and Williams are familiar with the various bar products Nestlé has produced over the years. They both remember well a bar called Sportsman's Chocolate Bracer. The bar was sold before and after World War II. It was similar in consistency to Army ration chocolate bars and held up well when the temperature was high. Sportsmen could carry the bar without worrying that they might melt during hunting, fishing, golfing, or whatever. The bar would be firm, ready, and waiting whenever a quick energy boost was needed.

L to R: Phil Williams, Harold Kenyon, and Curt Norpell

124

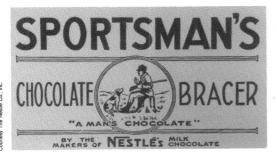

TRADE MARK REGISTERED
SPORTSMAN'S CHOCOLATE BRACER
"A MAN'S CHOCOLATE"

A sustaining bite of rich chocolate for quick energy.
Especially recommended for Athletes, Growing Children, Automobile and Picnic Parties.

Manufactured by
Peter Cailler Kohler Swiss Chocolates Co., Inc.
FULTON, NEW YORK, U. S. A.
NET WEIGHT 1⅜ OZ.   FIVE CENTS   NO. 205N

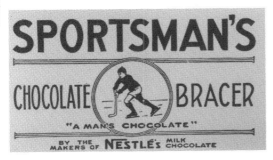

The Sportsman's wrapper had different illustrations on the front. One showed a fisherman with rod and reel and lures. Another showed a golfer, a hockey player, and so forth.

Nestlé bars from the 1960s include Fruit 'n Nut Bar, Peppermint Cream Bar, Caramel Cream Bar, and Triple Decker Bar. These are no longer produced.

In the early 1980s, the Nestlé Company decided to reformulate their American Nestlé bars by researching company records and coming as close as possible to the original milk chocolate formula invented by Henri Nestlé and Daniel Peter in 1875. In 1983, as a result, the Nestlé Milk Chocolate and Nestlé Milk Chocolate with Almonds bars were introduced to an appreciative American audience.

In late 1983, in addition to producing its already well-known line of candy bars, Nestlé acquired the candy lines produced by the Ward-Johnston Division of the Terson Company, Inc. Consequently, Nestlé now has added many time-honored names to its stable, including Chunky, Raisinets, Goobers, Sno-Caps, Bit-O-Honey, and Oh Henry!

The Brothers Runkel

Runkel Brothers, Inc., began operations in 1870 and soon became a prominent manufacturer of chocolate and cocoa in the United States. In 1905, the company applied for various trademarks, which were registered in 1906. Operating out of New York City, Runkel eventually opened a warehouse/office in Chicago. The Chicago operation supplied chocolate to such confectioners as Curtiss, Fannie May, and DeMets in Chicago. It consisted of a shipping room, office, and sales department.

The Chicago operation was located in the North Pier Terminal Building near the Navy Pier at the mouth of the Chicago River. Ships brought chocolate from the New York City factory through the Great Lakes. The chocolate came in huge blocks, which were hoisted up and through the big doors of the shipping room. From there, they were dispersed to fulfill orders.

A round chocolate bar called Headlights was sold as an unwrapped bar with the name Headlights impressed in it. It was similar in taste to the plain Hershey milk chocolate bar and was a good seller in the late 1920s and early 1930s.

Runkel Brothers was basically a chocolate supplier for confectioners, but they did make a line of chocolate bars in their New York factory that was sold to the general public. In the early 1920s, Runkel bars were listed in several regional candy maker catalogs. These bars were for sale in parts of the country where Runkel salespersons didn't operate. Some of the more popular Runkel bars were Milk Chocolate, Milk Chocolate with Almonds, and Sweet Milk Chocolate with Fruits and Nuts. Most of these bars had wrappers.

In 1937, Runkel Brothers went bankrupt. The machinery was bought by the National Equipment Corporation of New York City. Lamont, Corliss and Company, also of New York City, acquired the Runkel Brothers name and the trademarks, copyrights and trade secrets in 1938. In turn, the Nestlé Chocolate Company (presently The Nestlé Company, Inc.) has continued to use the formulas and information acquired from Runkel Brothers. Some of the trademarks are also used for some Nestlé products.

The Big Grind

During World War II, the mainstay bombers flown by the United States Army Air Force were the Consolidated B24 (Liberator) and the Boeing B17 (Flying Fortress). Both were four-engine planes equipped with various kinds of gun turrets.

The Flying Fortress was immortalized on a candy bar of the same name during the 1940s. It was manufactured by Walter Baker and Company, Ltd., of Dorchester, Massachusetts. The Flying Fortress bar was basically a civilian version of an Army ration chocolate bar that Walter Baker and Company was producing for the U. S. Army during World War II.

The first cocoa grinding operation in America was started in 1765 in Dorchester. John Hannon, a chocolate maker from Ireland, set up business in an old grist and saw mill with the financial aid of Dr. James Baker. Baker took over the business when Hannon and his ship were lost at sea on a mission to purchase cocoa beans in the West Indies in 1779.

In 1780, the mill's products were labeled Baker's Chocolate. By 1895, the business was incorporated as Walter Baker and Company. Walter was a grandson of Dr. Baker. In 1927, the company became a part of the General Foods Corporation and is now located in Delaware.

Baker's chocolate products make use of one of the oldest grocery product trademarks in America. In 1862, the president of the company was traveling in Europe and came across an intriguing painting in the Dresden Art Gallery in Germany. The painting, called La Belle Chocolatiere, had been hanging in the Dresden gallery for about one hundred years. It had been painted by a famous Swiss portrait painter, Jean Etienne Liotard.

The idea for the painting came in 1745, when an Austrian nobleman, Prince Ditrichstein, stopped in a shop in Vienna to try out a new chocolate drink being sold there. His waitress happened to be the daughter of an impoverished knight. The prince was smitten by the comely lass, and it wasn't long before she became Princess Ditrichstein. For one of her wedding gifts, the prince had her portrait painted by Liotard, who happened to be visiting Vienna at the time. The artist decided not to pose her in the formal dress of the time, but rather in a seventeenth-century costume. She posed as if she were serving chocolate.

The rest is history. When the Walter Baker and Company president saw the painting, he realized it would make a great trademark for Baker's Chocolate. By 1872, the Chocolate Girl was being used to advertise Baker's chocolate products.

Many Walter Baker and Company candy bars were produced in the 1940s along with the Flying Fortress bar. Some of them were Baker's Milk Chocolate with Hazelnuts, Baker's Semi-Sweet, Baker's Milk Chocolate with Malted Milk Crunch, Baker's Milk Chocolate, Milk Chocolate with Almonds, and Baker's Caracas Sweet Chocolate. The Caracas brand received its name from the capital city of Venezuela, where most of the cocoa beans were grown for this brand. No Baker candy bars are produced now.

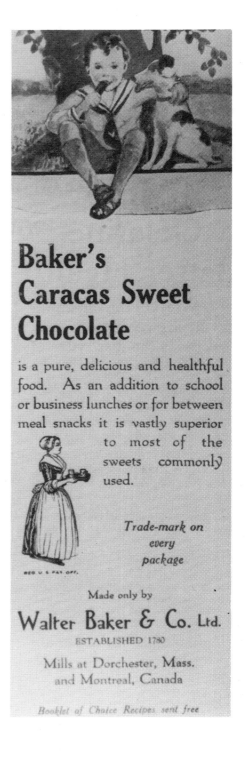

Baker's Caracas Sweet Chocolate

is a pure, delicious and healthful food. As an addition to school or business lunches or for between meal snacks it is vastly superior to most of the sweets commonly used.

Trade-mark on every package

Made only by

Walter Baker & Co. Ltd.

ESTABLISHED 1780

Mills at Dorchester, Mass. and Montreal, Canada

Booklet of Choice Recipes sent free

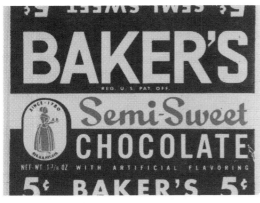

La Belle Chocolatiere, the Chocolate Girl, was on all the candy bar wrappers except the one for the Flying Fortress bar. The front of that wrapper carried a drawing of the B17, while the reverse carried a silhouette of the aircraft. For patriotic reasons, the Chocolate Girl stepped aside that one time.

Winner from Day One

Already a successful candy manufacturer in New York City, Sol Leaf in 1921 was lured to Chicago by family ties. There he built a candy company on the vacant lot owned by his wife's sister, founding the Overland Candy Company.

There was no real significance to the name Overland. In fact, Sol was known to change the name from Overland Candy Company or Corporation one day to Sol S. Leaf, Chicago, Illinois, the next. Other company names Sol used over the years were Marshall and Norman Candy Company, Chicago Biscuit and Cone Company, Dietz

Gum Company, and Simple Simon Candy Company. By changing labels and boxes to fill orders, he was always sure of getting a better-than-average share of the market. It wasn't until 1947 that the name Leaf Brands was adopted for the company. Presently, it's known as Leaf, Inc., a division of the Huhtamaki Group, a Finnish pharmaceuticals and food firm.

The first product of Overland Candy was a marshmallow confection inserted in a baked cone, simulating an ice cream cone. By the mid-1930s, the company could have been described as a combination of a general line candy company, a biscuit company producing sugar wafers, and a chewing gum company. Leaf was one of the first gum companies to package different series of trading cards in packets of their bubble gum.

Candy bars were part of the Leaf line in years past. In the late 1920s and early 1930s, two of the candy bars produced under the Overland name were the Overland Bar and the You Bet bar. The Overland Bar was marketed through vending machines operated by Automatic Canteen Company of America. Wrappers from the Overland Bar, along with other candy bars carrying the Canteen coupon on the label, could be redeemed for premiums offered at the offices of the Canteen Company in Merchandise Mart in Chicago.

The You Bet bar carried the subhead, "0¢-1¢-2¢ no higher!" on each wrapper. The bar was one of the many offered by numerous candy companies as prizes on punchboards in neighborhood variety stores and other locations. Another punchboard candy bar was produced under the Sol S. Leaf imprint. Called the SirPrize Egg bar, its wrapper said, "Be surprised! 1¢ to 5¢." The various cent figures on the wrappers indicated the cost of each punch taken from the board.

Other former Leaf bars had delightful names. There was the five-cent Happy Harry bar; the 12 O'Clock Bar—"Good All The Time"; and a bar called King Solomon, "A Wise Bar." The latter two were also good nickel sellers for a number of years.

In the 1960s, two bars were produced—Malteser, and Sanwich, a milk chocolate-covered caramel wafer bar. Both these bars were ten-cent items. Fore was another ten-cent item. Brunch was a five-cent bar. And there was even a Playboy Bunny Chocolate that sold for a dime.

No doubt about it, Sol Leaf was a real winner in his day. He constantly pursued greater knowledge when it came to the candy industry, which was his only hobby. His spirit lives on, because it was his example as a winner that has kept the company moving at a merry pace.

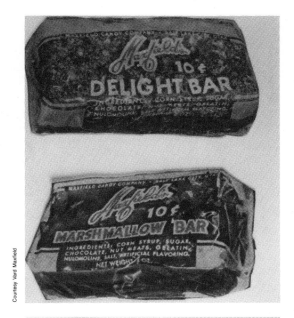

Courtesy Vard Maxfield

Courtesy Vard Maxfield

Logs Are More Than Just Lumber

In 1947, the Maxfield Candy Company of Salt Lake City got into the ten-cent candy bar business when Vard Maxfield and two partners decided to make a go of it.

Vard had learned the trade at the Glade Candy Company in Salt Lake City, where he started working in 1934. He was still with Glade when the president of the company found out that Verd was contemplating starting his own operation. The president promptly fired him.

As a result, Maxfield and his two partners went into business for themselves sooner than anticipated. Their first candy bar was issued in November, 1947. They broadened their line the next year, producing a Nut Fudge bar, a Marshmallow Bar, and an Opera Bar. Another, called the Delight Bar, had a layered chocolate/vanilla/strawberry marshmallow center and was both colorful and tasty when served sliced.

Later bars were Cherry-Ett, Golden Glo, and the good-selling Fruit and Nut Bar. After selling decently for a number of years, all these bars were discontinued, because manufacturing techniques were creating production problems. Other candy lines, though, such as saltwater taffy, were continued.

In recent years, a gourmet line of bars has been started with bars such as Cashew Log, Caramel Log, Pecan Log, and Vanilla and Chocolate Fudge Logs. These logs, by the way, appeal to others besides lumberjacks.

The Road for Sam Wasn't Rocky

Sam Altshuler came to the United States from Russia. He was penniless and had no knowledge of the English language. As a result, he took the first job offered him. And as sweet luck would have it, the job was that of a candy maker's helper.

Sam was a quick learner and found out all he could about the candy business. Then he set out on his own. But World War II came along, and the candy business had to wait while Sam worked in shipyards during the war.

By 1950, Sam founded the Annabelle

Candy Company, Inc., named after his daughter, who is now president and chairman of the board. In 1951, the Rocky Road candy bar was first produced in the company factory in San Francisco. In 1965, a new plant was opened in Hayward, California, and Altshuler also purchased the Golden Nugget Candy Company.

In 1978, the Cardinet Candy Company was purchased from Ralston Purina. At the Concord, California, factory, the U-No, U-No Mint, and Abba-Zaba bars are now produced.

The Cardinet Company was founded in 1906. It was headquartered in Oakland, California, with factories in San Francisco and Los Angeles. It first produced an almond nougat bar and then Texas Tommy, a chocolate-coated marshmallow and peanut candy that appeared late in 1911. The two were popular in West Coast baseball parks until 1920, when Cardinet's Baffle Bar was first produced. One of Cardinet's best sellers, the Baffle Bar, was "pure cream, crisp nuts, and rich chocolate." A slogan for that bar, copyrighted in 1923, said, "Take one home/slice it."

To introduce the bar nationally, ads were placed in magazines such as *The Saturday Evening Post.* If you couldn't find the Baffle Bar in your neighborhood, you could ". . .send 50¢ to us for a box of five 10¢ Baffle Bars. . .approximately a pound of the most delicious candy that can be bought anywhere. We prepay postage in the U.S. . . .Use the coupon."

Courtesy Alan Bitterman

Before Annabelle acquired it, the Golden Nugget Candy Company was a division of the Reed Candy Company. Big Hunk, Look, and Sir were name bars produced by that company, which also handled Charleston Chew! in the Western states in the 1960s.

Sadly, the Baffle Bar and other old Cardinet favorites such as Night Editor, Hot-Air, Nob Hill, Co-Co Nut, and Student Prince are no longer being made. But perhaps the Baffle Bar will be reintroduced someday.

At the Hayward plant today, Annabelle Rocky Roads are produced, as are Rocky Road Mint, Butterscotch Coated Rocky Road, Look, and Big Hunk. Discontinued Annabelle bars include Sir, Taffy Treat, Colossal, Full of Almonds, Brazil Nut, and Mambo, which was named after a dance craze.

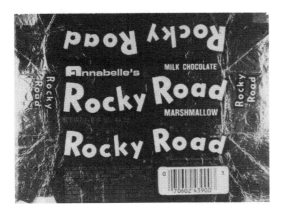

Sam Altshuler came a long way in the candy business in a relatively few years. He found that the road wasn't at all rocky when he began making his own Rocky Road.

Skokie Herb

Having a problem producing candy bars? Chocolate products? Anything at all along candy lines? If so, the person to go to with your problem is Herb Knechtel of the Chicago suburb of Skokie, Illinois.

Knechtel runs Knechtel Research Sciences Inc., which acts as a consultant to the candy industry by researching problems and coming up with solutions. Suppose, for instance, a confectioner wanted to come out with a new candy bar incorporating chocolate, apricots, and other ingredients. Knechtel would go through the actual production stages, using a laboratory that is a candy factory in miniature. As a result of analyzing all aspects of production this way, many world-famous candies have emerged from the Knechtel laboratory.

Knechtel, a native of Moose Jaw, Saskatchewan, grew up with several sisters, but he became the fudge maker in the family. In 1927, he left for Seattle, Washington, where he worked for the Robinettes candy chain. In 1928, he was working for a gentleman who was trying to acquire trade secrets from other confectionery companies. This man sent Knechtel on missions throughout the country. Knechtel would get a job at a candy plant, learn the plant's secrets, and then quit after a few days so he could move on to the next company and the next batch of secrets.

One of the plants Knechtel visited as a "spy" was run by a man named Overhauser in Oakland, California. An excellent candy bar called Trail Toffee was produced in the factory, and Knechtel tried to gain access to the locked room containing the formula and the machines that produced the bar. Knechtel was unsuccessful except for one quick peek at the machinery. Overhauser died a few weeks after Knechtel left the company, and he took the recipe with him to the grave.

But over the years, Knechtel managed to duplicate the bar in his laboratory. Some of the wrappers are labeled H.K. 25. The 25 means it took Knechtel twenty-five years to work out the formula. Consisting of high-quality ingredients, the bar is now distributed by When Candy Was Candy, Inc., of Libertyville, Illinois.

By the time Knechtel was twenty-two, he owned five retail candy stores and a factory in Seattle. During the Depression, however, he went broke and lost it all.

In 1933, Knechtel convinced the management of a supermarket chain in Portland, Oregon, that candy could be sold in grocery stores. He quickly became a success at doing just that, and as a result, in 1941, he was hired by Marshall Field's of Chicago to run their candy division.

Between 1941 and 1954, Knechtel developed much of the Marshall Field candy line, including that company's best-known candy creation, the Frango mint. The mint was developed in 1945, just as World War II ended. Knechtel realized that the public was hungry for good chocolate after the imitations during the war years.

Chocolate was still scarce in 1945, so Knechtel went to a chocolate company and convinced the owner to sell him all the milk chocolate on hand. Two truck-loads of milk chocolate were brought back to Field's, where the other employees figured Knechtel had gone overboard. But Knechtel persisted and produced the almost 100 percent chocolate Frango mints. The mints were introduced in full-page newspaper ads with the headline, "Real Chocolate Is Back." Sales were limited to one box per customer, but they sold out quickly. From then on, Frango mints became a fixture in the Midwest. Today the Frango mint is available in bar form in several flavors in addition to the original mint.

Originally, the mints were going to be called Franco, but that name was too similar to Francisco Franco, the Spanish leader who wasn't too popular in the United States at the time. The substitute name of Frango was borrowed from a candy made by Fredrick and Nelson, a Seattle department store owned by Field's.

Knechtel left Field's in 1954 to open his consulting firm, the first such company to serve the confectionery industry.

Because of Knechtel's incredible knowledge about the candy business, he has become a legend in his own time and deserves recognition as a good-will ambassador for the entire confectionery industry. (By the way, that HK-25 bar of Skokie Herb's tastes mighty good.)

Rhumba King

Think of the rhumba and who comes to mind? None other than Xavier Cugat. During the late 1940s, he produced a Cugats Nugat Bar that was distributed by L. R. Stone Company, Inc., of Los Angeles, California. One section of the wrapper read, "Xavier Cugat, The Rhumba King, is the world-famous orchestra leader, Metro Goldwyn-Mayer motion picture star, Columbia recording artist, radio network artist, world-famous cartoonist, popularizer of the rhumba, and now a candymaker. . . ."

The wrapper also featured a message about a songwriting contest. Cugat had written a new rhumba, which he called "Cugats Nugats." But he had no words to the tune, so he invited the public to write the lyrics. By sending in a stamped, self-addressed reply envelope, contestants could obtain rules to win the one-thousand-dollar grand prize or one of the two hundred eighty-five other prizes offered. All contestants had to do was write the best words to go along with the tune.

Another legend on the wrapper said that if you sent along two wrappers, ten cents, and a stamped, self-addressed envelope, you would receive a booklet by Cugat that would teach you in easy, under-standable lessons how to properly and expertly do the rhumba, the tango, and the samba. Also included with the book would be a list of premiums given away with Cugats Nugat candy bar wrappers!

In Cugat's book, *Rhumba Is My Life*, published in 1948 by Didier in New York, Cugat said he had a large financial stake in Cugats Nugat. When Cugat was in California before World War II, John L. Stone asked him to go into the candy business. Stone had been successful growing fruits and nuts. The war postponed the partnership, but after the war, Cugats Nugat bar was launched. In his book, Cugat said the bar was produced in all fruit flavors, plus rum. Cugat also said that when the popular radio commentator Walter Winchell heard of the candy bar Cugat was producing, he remarked, "I always knew he was nutty."

Cugat went on to say, "To commemorate my venture into the candy business, I composed and introduced a new rhumba." What Cugat didn't mention in his book was whether or not he ever found suitable lyrics for the rhumba from the entries in the prize contest offered on his candy bar wrapper.

Cugat was a true showman. It's too bad his venture into the candy business didn't set the world on fire.

Washington Square

To celebrate the centenary of George Washington's inauguration, New York City in 1889 erected a temporary wood and plaster memorial arch in Washington Square, at the southern tip of Fifth Avenue. Stanford White, the noted architect, designed it. The temporary arch was so favorably viewed by the public that a private committee was soon formed to raise money for a permanent arch. Ignace Paderewski even staged a benefit concert at the Metropolitan Opera and donated the $4,500 gate receipts to the building fund. The arch is of white marble and was finished in 1892. It was turned over to the city in 1895 after the construction costs had been paid off.

In the 1940s, the P. Margarella Company honored the arch by introducing their Washington Square Mint Pattie. The wrapper pictured the George Washington memorial arch. Margarella also produced its own Margarella Mint and a number of bars labeled Forestwood, including the Forestwood Wonder Bar and a Forestwood Marshmallow Bar. Another Margarella bar was named Forestwood Flash, and its wrapper showed a lightning bolt. The name might have evolved from the popular comic book character, Superman.

The P. Margarella Company no longer exists, but an arch it once honored on one of its candy bar wrappers still stands. The lesson here must be that marble stands up better over time than does a mint pattie.

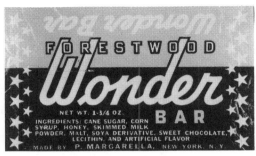

Give a Whistle

Walter Lowney started in the candy business in Boston in 1880. He soon was producing Philadelphia caramels, other candy products, and even some hand-made chocolate bars. Shortly after the turn of the century his candy factory, located on Washington Street in Boston, was providing work for many neighborhood employees turning out chocolate bars such as Medallion.

LOWNEY BROS. & CO.,
FINE CONFECTIONERY,
Original Philadelphia Caramels,
500 Washington Street, Boston.

Edmund Littler, a Canadian, began to import Lowney products into Canada in 1896. In 1906 Littler and Lowney built a manufacturing plant in Montreal. Littler and Lowney became a Canadian company in 1924.

A plant in Mansfield, Massachusetts, which once was a Lowney chocolate factory, now makes Welch's Chocolate Covered Cherries and Merckens Chocolate, operating as a division of Nabisco Brands.

While located in Boston, Lowney produced many candy bars during the 1920s and early 1930s, including the popular Hey Eddie candy bar. One of the cherished prizes that could be obtained by buying Hey Eddie bars was a round, metal whistle. To make it work kids inhaled rather than blowing into it. (Those whistles that were worth only a penny back then, sell for around $30 today!)

There's More in Cincinnati Than Just WKRP

That zany cast on WKRP, Cincinnati, put Cincinnati on the TV program map. But there's more to this genial city on the Ohio and home of the old Big Red Machine.

In 1902, for example, a new candy first tickled the taste buds of Cincinnati candy lovers. It came from Doscher's Candies and was named French Chew.

John Doscher, Sr., was another of those candymen who immigrated from Germany. He came over in 1865 and learned the candy trade working with other family members.

By 1871 he had opened his own candy plant. He and his co-workers produced all kinds of candy, all appreciated by the good burghers of Cincinnati. But it wasn't until 1902 that Doscher's reputation was established as a premier candy maker. That's when French Chew appeared for the first time. A combination of whipped and hard candy, French Chew was sold in bulk and piece form until 1950, when it came out as a nougat candy bar.

CRACK and CHEW

Several other candy bars were made by Doscher's in the 1950s, but they didn't stay on the scene too long. The Goober Cluster was made from 1954 to 1957. And the Nut Burger was first made in 1956, but was never put into full production.

The French Chew bar, available in vanilla, strawberry, and chocolate, is still going strong. A nougat candy bar, it holds up well in all kinds of weather. Basically available only in a few states near Cincinnati, it deserves a wider audience. Let's hear it for John Doscher, Sr. The company he founded is now called the French Chew Candy Company, named for his most successful confection.

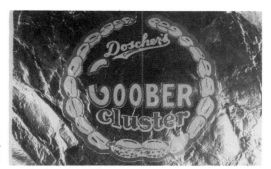

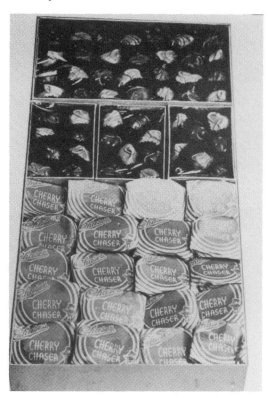

"Mr. Chase, Come Here. I Want You."

The year 1876 had numerous high-lights, such as the introduction of Hire's Root Beer Extract, Heinz Tomato Ketchup, and Budweiser Beer.

The Battle of the Little Big Horn came to a climax when the U. S. Seventh Cavalry under General George Armstrong Custer was wiped out by Indian forces led by Chiefs Sitting Bull and Crazy Horse.

It was also in 1876 when Alexander Graham Bell transmitted the first complete spoken sentences over wire when he said, "Mr. Watson, come here. I want you." Had Bell been talking to someone just starting in the confectionery business, he might have said either, "Mr. Chase, come here. I want you." Or, "Mr. Bunte, come here, I want you." Why so? Because the Chase Candy Company (started by George Washington Chase) and Bunte Brothers Candy Company (started by Ferdinand and Gustave Bunte) both began in 1876. Chase was in St. Joseph, Missouri, and Bunte Brothers was in Chicago. Strange as it may seem, in 1954 the two compa-nies became one without any planning on the part of the founders.

The Chase company was family owned until 1944, when it was sold to F. S. Yan-tis and Company, an investment broker-age group in Chicago. Before it was sold, the Chase plant made everything from two-for-a-penny items to a ten-pound box of chocolates featured on punchboards. Chase made many candy bars at the time, but only a few were paired with punchboards. They included Cherry Chaser and assorted sizes of Pecan Bars. The five-cent Cherry Chaser bar was simi-lar to the popular Cherry Mash bar that Chase produced for over-the-counter sales.

The well-known Chase Candy Cop was prominently featured on candy bar wrappers as well as on the front of Chase catalogs. Some favorite Chase candy bars of the late 1920s and early 1930s were Pierce Arrow, Casey Jones, Mallo Milk, Nutrol, Black Walnut, Malted Milk, Chasenut Bar, 'Tween Meals, and Candy Dogs.

Upon the Yantis takeover, Chase began a series of acquisitions that within a few years made it one of the giants of the confectionery business. In 1946, the National Candy Company was purchased from Clinton Foods of Clinton, Iowa. National had been founded by V. L. Price, a gentleman instrumental in the formation of the National Confectioners Association and the organization's first president. (His son, by the way, became the well-known motion picture star, Vincent Price.)

At one time, National had twenty-two plants across the country. The major plants were located in Chicago and St. Louis. National made a general line of candy and such candy bars as Bob Cat and Hippo. Soon after National was acquired, Chase headquarters were moved to the St. Louis plant.

The O'Brien Candy Company of San Jose, California, was bought in 1948 from an old California family that dated back in that state to the Gold Rush days. O'Brien was noted for its candies packed in tins. During World War II, those tins were sold by the hundreds of thousands for use by the military in the tropical areas where U.S. troops fought in the South Pacific. After the war, O'Brien

began advertising nationally. The now well-known O'Brien's Almond Butter

141

Crunch was offered for sale in tins, as advertised by "Señor O'Brien, the Candy Cabellero from California."

The Shotwell Candy Company of Chicago was bought in 1952 and soon liquidated. Shotwell had made an extensive line of candy bars, including Red Grange, Strongheart, and Big Yank. It also produced Puritan, a well-known brand of marshmallows. Only the Puritan marshmallow was continued after Shotwell was acquired by Chase. That was perhaps all to the good, because some former Shotwell managers were found guilty of violating federal price control laws established during the shortage period of World War II.

Chase purchased the Nutrine Candy Company of Chicago in 1951. A general line house, its principle assets were several top-flight candy salesmen. While in business, Nutrine was often the butt of rival companies' jokes. "Did you say Nutrine Candy Company or Latrine Candy Company?"

In 1954, Chase made its biggest move by acquiring Bunte Brothers Candy Company. Bunte had established itself as one of the top candy makers in the United States. The company made a general line of candy as well as candy bars. A number of confectioners who later made names for themselves got their start at Bunte. They included George Williamson (Oh Henry!), Emil Brach (Brach Candies), and J. R. Holloway (Milk Duds).

With the consolidation of Chase and Bunte, operations in St. Louis were closed, and general offices and manufacturing moved to the Bunte Building in Chicago. The corporate name became Bunte Brothers-Chase Candy Company.

Some of the candy bars Bunte featured over the years were Toddle, Spanish Peanut Bar, Pippin, Super-Five, Chocolate Creamy Cakes, and its best-known bar, Tangos. Tangos bars were first marketed by Bunte Brothers in 1914. Originally oval in shape, they were changed to an oblong when vending machines began making inroads into the distribution of bars.

Until the spring of 1956, Tangos were coated in dark chocolate only. After that, they were milk-chocolate covered. The bar had a heavy maple cream base topped with white, vanilla-flavored whipped marshmallow, and it contained an ample amount of roasted peanuts.

In the early 1960s, the Tangos bar was a ten-cent item before finally fading from the scene. Chase still holds rights to the Tangos bar, so perhaps some day it will resurrect this classic candy.

The Bunte-Chase plant was closed in 1961, and Chase operated as the Chase General Corporation out of St. Joseph. The Bunte name was sold to the Walter Williams Candy Company of Oklahoma City, which changed its name to Bunte Candies, Inc.

Chase then bought Poe Candy Company in St. Joseph and the Dye Candy Company in Eldon, Missouri. Chase closed both those plants to consolidate manufacturing in the Chase plant built in St. Joseph in 1963.

The Chase Peanut Cluster bar was introduced in 1975 as a companion bar to the popular Cherry Mash, which came out as a five-cent number in 1916 and sold for ten cents at the start of World War II. It's still a best seller in the Midwest today and is the number-one product of the Chase and Poe Candy Companies, with Bill Yantis in charge.

The Ma Bell operation that evolved from what Alexander Graham Bell started is no longer an entity today. But that which George Washington Chase started is still going strong. Perhaps that's an omen that the candy bar is indeed more powerful than the machine.

Just for Fun

Kids of the Thirties

Kids are born collectors. And for kids interested in sports in the 1930s, the thing to do was to collect baseball cards. If you were lucky, you had a few of those old Sweet Caporal, Piedmont, or other cigarette company baseball cards given to you by an uncle or older brother. Or you might even be lucky enough to have some of the cards that had been premiums in boxes of Cracker Jack.

It was 1933 when the world of collecting baseball cards opened up for kids who had just a penny or two to spend. That's when the Goudey Gum Company of Boston issued its first set of Big League cards. The DeLong Gum Company of Boston also issued a set of cards, but Big League was the better seller. That was the beginning of a hobby that today attracts kids and adults alike. Topps, Fleers, and Donruss are now the big guns.

Baseball, the Goudey Gum Company, and the Bit-O-Honey candy bar all play parts in the following three tales about growing up in the Great Depression.

The South Boulevard Alley Cats

Growing up in the Midwest in the 1930's was a wonderful experience despite the Depression—especially if you were a kid in my neighborhood in Evanston, Illinois. Why? Because that's when and where the South Boulevard Alley Cats did their thing.

The main street in our neighborhood was called South Boulevard. Behind the street was an alley where garbage and trash was placed, and where homeowners had access to their garages. Many of the yards had fences that backed up to the alley, and those fences were natural gathering places for all the neighborhood cats. On moonlit evenings, those cats would really put on a concert. There would be solo howling, howling in three-part harmony, yodeling, and snarling, among other things. Those cats proved to be a tough, rough, and mean bunch.

It was natural, then, that neighborhood kids picked the nickname Alley Cats for their baseball team. Every kid who wasn't yet in high school was eligible for membership.

Our team captain was our best hitter, best fielder, best pitcher, and the fastest runner by far. The captain was also the toughest, meanest kid in the neighborhood. Her name was Catharine.

It didn't bother the boys one bit that the team captain was a girl. Nor did it bother them that the second baseman was a girl, too. She was the sister of Johnny May, our catcher. The sister had a first name, but Johnny always called her "Sister," so that's what we called her, too. Sister was nearly as good a hitter as Catharine was, and she also could hold her own as a fielder.

The one potential klutz on the team was one of our substitutes, Eugene. He didn't approach klutzhood lightly. No, he went at it full steam. Now there's nothing wrong with wearing glasses, which Eugene did. The problem is that he'd almost always forget to wear them when we played ball. That's why he'd often get hit on top of

TINKER, Chicago - Federals

CHANCE, CHICAGO NAT'L

the head by fly balls. He made Babe Herman, the major league funny man in the 1930s, look like a ballet dancer.

Eugene also used to stumble over his own feet. As his mom used to say, "Eugene is growing rapidly. He's awkward for his age." In truth, Eugene was awkward for almost all ages.

Even though Eugene almost always struck out and made all kinds of errors, we still liked him. I guess we thought of him as a ten-year-old imitation of Harold Lloyd, the popular movie comedian of the times.

In the 1930s, adults didn't organize sports for kids. We did it all ourselves. We supplied our own umpires. We used our own balls, liberally wrapped in yards of friction tape when the original covers flew off in a million shredded pieces. We used our own bats, many of them cracked and held together with nails, tacks, and more yards of friction tape.

We also made our own ball field in an empty lot on the corner of South Boulevard and Asbury Street—almost the dead center of the neighborhood. And then we had to find other neighborhood teams to play against.

One of our arch rivals was an Oakton Street team from the other side of Ridge Avenue. We'd play them two or three times a year. Each game would take a whole day for the visiting team, who would have to walk miles to and from the game.

On the morning of one of those games, Catharine got mad because our regular center fielder had a stomach ache and couldn't play. That meant I had to switch over from right field, my regular position, to play center. And Eugene, our klutz substitute, would play right field.

Catharine made sure Eugene had his glasses before the game started. Even so, he made four errors during the game. He was the reason the Oakton Street team was ahead by one run when we came up for our last bats in the ninth.

Johnny was the first batter and got a

single, but the next batter hit into a double play. Two out already. Just one more and the game was over. And the next batter was Eugene. He'd been up four times already and had struck out each time.

We all moaned when Eugene swung and missed the first pitch. And the second. But on the third, the pitcher wound up and let the ball fly. He wanted to finish the game in a hurry, but the pitch was wild.

"Duck, Eugene!" we all hollered.

I guess Eugene wasn't listening. He wasn't even really watching the ball. He was too busy starting to swing his bat, which was why the ball hit him on the shoulder.

Catharine jumped up and down. "You got hit by the ball! You got hit by the ball! You get up to go to first base, Eugene! Whoopee!"

Eugene had a big smile on his face as he trotted down to first.

Catharine pounded me on the back. "Okay. It's up to you now," she shouted. "Grab a bat and get up to the plate and get a hit!" The pitcher stomped back to the mound. He was itching to get me out in a hurry.

Well I was no dumb kid, so I started thinking. I was small to begin with. And if I crouched real low in the batter's box, maybe I'd get a walk. Then both Eugene and I would be on base when Catharine came up to bat.

I got set at the plate and wiggled down low. The pitcher let fly. The pitch came in way over my head.

"Ball one," the umpire hollered.

Eugene was jumping up and down on first. He yelled something to the pitcher that I didn't quite hear, but the pitcher stuck out his tongue at Eugene. Eugene whooped and bounced up and down even more.

The pitcher gritted his teeth and winged in the next pitch, which sailed over the head of the catcher!

For once in his life, Eugene didn't do

anything wrong. He broke for second base and slid into the bag before the catcher could even retrieve the ball. When the catcher did find it, he threw the ball past the second baseman into center field.

Eugene got up quickly and went to third. The center fielder, in a hurry to field the ball, was off balance and made a bad toss to third. Eugene just kept on going and rounded third base. The third baseman ran after the bad throw and then zoomed the ball to the catcher.

By now everyone on our team was screaming and hollering because Eugene and the ball were both headed for home, and it seemed as if they would both arrive at the same second.

So what did Eugene do? He tripped! He tripped just six feet from home and from scoring the tying run.

But the catcher was caught by surprise. While he was watching Eugene tripping and falling all over himself, the ball bonked him on top of the head and bounced off down the first-base line.

Eugene saw what was happening as he was stretched out on the ground. But he was so pooped from all the running he'd done, he crawled the last six feet to the plate.

After he touched home, we all jumped and hollered. Some of us even pounded Eugene on the back as he lay over home plate. Eugene had scored the tying run!

Everyone crowded around Eugene to shake his hand after he got up. Even Catharine gave him a big smile and a bear hug. For once, Eugene was a real hero.

We finally managed to win the ball game because I scored on a ball that Catharine hit over the left fielder's head. But the real hero of the ball game was our klutz, Eugene. After the game, we all chipped in to buy Eugene an Eskimo Pie—a chocolate-covered vanilla ice cream bar—at Decker's Store.

Eugene only got two licks off his Eskimo Pie, though. As he went out the door, he tripped, and the bar scooted across the sidewalk and into the gutter.

We all laughed. Eugene was his old self again.

Root Beer Extract

In the 1930s, everyone in our neighborhood had hobbies. And if you played on the South Boulevard Alley Cats, you had at least three hobbies. One of them was playing baseball, of course. A second was cheering for a favorite major league baseball team. Since we lived just outside Chicago, we had two choices—the Cubs or the White Sox. Most of us were Cubs fans, except for a few like Eugene and Johnny.

Our third hobby was collecting baseball cards. It began in 1933, when the Goudey Gum Company issued its first set of Big League baseball cards. For a penny, you got one baseball card and a slab of brownish-gray stuff called gum, all in a colorful wrapper. As I recollect, that gum had a god-awful flavor and texture—something like chewy shoe leather spiced with essence of spearmint or wintergreen.

You only stuck the slab into your mouth if you were desperate. Otherwise, the gum was quickly discarded along with the wrapper. Eugene saved his slabs, however. His Dad used the gum to caulk windows in their house.

The only important thing in the package was the baseball card. And what a prize you had if your purchase turned out to be a Cub player like Guy Bush or Billy Herman. Of course, once you got a Cub, you hung onto it for dear life. You never traded a Cub Card—not even a duplicate. Doing so would be disloyal to the cause.

Collecting baseball cards in those days wasn't easy, because money was pretty tight. At the most, we only had two or three pennies to spend each week for candy. And one of those pennies was always spent on "eating candy," such as bull's-eyes or Mary Janes or banana squares. "Eating candy" made up for the yucky Goudey gum slabs.

So how did we ever manage to get new Cubbies? Well, Eugene was our answer. First of all, Eugene liked the White Sox, not the Cubs. And Eugene had a rich grandfather. Each Friday night, Eugene got a buffalo nickel from his granddad, who came to supper. They always had fish on Friday night since the family was Catholic. Eugene got his nickel after he took the fish bones out to the garbage can when the meal was over.

First thing on Saturday, a few of us would be waiting around Eugene's house to walk the block and a half to Decker's store with him. We'd watch as he handed the nickel to Mr. Decker.

Mr. Decker had little white paper bags that were used for gum and candy. He'd fill one bag with five packs of Big League gum, then hand the bag to Eugene.

We crowded around Eugene outside Decker's as he slowly opened each pack. We'd "oh" and "ah" as each card appeared and was passed around and admired. We read the legend on the back of each of the cards with reverence.

On one of those Saturdays, just Eugene and I went to Decker's. I had an extra penny that day, so I bought one pack, too. My card pictured Ted Lyons, probably the best White Sox pitcher at the time. Ted was also Eugene's idol. His eyes bugged when he saw the card. To his chagrin, he got no White Soxers, but he did get two Cubbies—Babe Herman and Kiki Cuyler.

When I saw those two Cubbies, I began to drool. I'll give you my Ted Lyons for those two," I quickly said.

Well, even though Eugene was a klutz, he certainly hadn't been behind the barn door when the brains were passed out. He just smiled and shook his head slowly.

"Nope," he said. "Just one for one. But I'll make a deal for the other one."

"What kind of deal?" I asked.

"I've got to do something for my mom this morning. I don't want to miss ball practice, so if you help me I'll give you the other card."

Who could turn down a proposition like that?

Eugene's morning project was to put caps on a batch of bottles of homemade root beer. His dad had made the batch the day before using Hires Root Beer Extract, yeast, and water. They had just bought a new-fangled capping machine that put metal caps on the bottles. But Eugene didn't know exactly how to work the thing, so he grabbed a handful of old corks from a box on a basement shelf. He handed some of the corks to me to stop up the brown and green bottles.

"Jam the corks in good and tight," Eugene told me. "We don't want to let any of that root beer leak out."

Eugene supposedly knew what he was doing, so I followed directions and jammed corks into the bottles, good and tight.

After we finished the cork jamming, Eugene said to shake up the bottles so as to mix up the yeast that had settled on the bottom. So we shook. I still didn't think Eugene knew what he was talking about, but who was I to question his orders when I was to get that Babe Herman card for my efforts?

With the last bottle shaken, we left the house for the ball field. The rest of the Alley Cats were already winging the ball around getting ready for the game that afternoon. It took us just a few seconds to reach the field because it was right across the street from Eugene's house.

We had been practicing for about half an hour when we began to hear funny noises.

"Sounds like somebody's shooting off a Daisy BB gun," Eugene said.

"Yep," I answered. Sometimes it even sounds like a cannon going off."

Eugene kind of squinted as he said, "And it sounds like it's coming from my house."

Just then Eugene's mom came flying out the front door. "Eugene!" she hollered. "Get over here quick. I think the whole basement is blowing up!"

Eugene rushed across the street, with me right behind him. As we got closer to the house, I recognized the noises.

I grabbed Eugene by the arm. "Down in the basement. I think I know what's happening. Let's go down and see."

Eugene looked startled. "No way," he muttered. "Who wants to get blown up? My mom knows what she's talking about."

I managed to drag him over to one of the basement windows and I peered in.

What a mess! Many of the corks had popped out of the bottles and root beer was foaming all over the floor. Other bottles had burst with the corks still jammed in the necks, leaving broken glass in the root beer sea.

I finally got Eugene to look in the window. Just as he put his eyes up to the glass, one of the corks came zinging out of a bottle and crashed through the window, just missing Eugene's ear.

"Wow!" he yelled. "Guess we did something wrong, huh?"

That was the understatement of 1933. I later found out that the yeast was *supposed* to settle at the bottom of the bottles. And you never shook a corked bottle, especially if the cork had been jammed in. Otherwise you ended up with what in later years became known as a Molotov cocktail.

Eugene's mom ran out of the house again. By now she knew what had happened. She grabbed Eugene by the ear and dragged him into the house. "What a son," she complained. "Always making trouble. At least the house isn't blowing up. But you're going down into that basement right now to clean up all that mess. No more ball playing until it's done, you hear me?"

Eugene was dejected as the screen door slammed behind him. His ear must have been sore, too—his mom didn't let go until she had propelled him back down into the basement.

I let out a slow whistle as I walked back to the ball field. I really felt sorry for Eugene, now that he would be spending the rest of the morning cleaning up the root beer mess.

But it didn't make me less jubilant. After all, I had the Babe Herman card safely in my back pocket.

The First American Rocket Program

Aviation was the coming thing in the early 1930s. Every kid on the block wanted to be a pilot. And that included everyone in the South Boulevard neighborhood—even Catharine. She had gotten a leather pilot helmet like Charles Lindbergh's from her dad, and she wore it every day for a whole week, including Sunday. Finally her mom put her foot down. "No wearing that thing to mass— no way! If you keep that darn thing on your head twenty-four hours a day, your hair won't get any air and pretty soon it will all drop out. Now you wouldn't want that, would you?"

Of course Catharine didn't want all her hair to drop out. After all, who ever heard of a hairless girl who was captain of a baseball team? Catharine traded the helmet to Eugene for a Little Orphan Annie decoder ring that Eugene had received for sending in a seal from an Ovaltine can to the Little Orphan Annie radio program.

Eugene's mother, too, laid down the law to him about his wearing the new pilot's helmet. It wasn't allowed at meals or in bed. In fact, he could only wear it when he was playing outside or was inside listening to "The Air Adventures of Jimmie Allen" on the radio. The show was produced in Chicago and first hit the airwaves in 1933. The Chicago area sponsor was the Skelly Gas Company, so Jimmie

Allen pins, books, and other premiums were available at local Skelly gas stations. We all begged our dads to pull into Skelly stations, buy some gas for the old flivver, and bring home a Jimmie Allen premium or two.

Jimmie Allen was a young daredevil pilot in the rather shaky days of early aviation. In time, the show became popular in syndication, and more than three million kids joined Jimmie Allen Flying Clubs. Those kids all had great dreams of one day piloting such beauties as Jimmie flew on dangerous missions around the world and in competition in intercontinental air races.

Our nearest Skelly gas station operator even opened a local branch of the Jimmie Allen Flying Club. We could get credit on a punched card for gasoline purchased by our dads. When your card was completely punched, you were eligible for a free Saturday morning movie in the summer at the Coronet Theater.

Jimmie Allen

In the first (and only) Jimmie Allen Movie Safari, the operator took almost all the South Boulevard Alley Cats, plus an assortment of other youngsters, to the theater. There were about thirty of us.

The trip started out well, but after the three-mile trek in 90-degree heat, our tongues were hanging out. The Skelly operator bought each of us a soda pop at a nickel a head. He had only promised us a nickel's worth of candy, but he didn't want a bunch of dehydrated kids on his hands, so he popped for the drinks, too. Eugene downed his Double Cola, and the operator gave each of us a nickel for candy.

Eugene was cagy. He had also brought thirty cents saved from the money his grandfather gave him. And what did he do? He bought seven boxes of Holloway's Milk Duds and took them inside the theater with him. And believe it or not, he chewed up all those Milk Duds during the fifteen-minute Flash Gordon serial that ran first.

The Saturday feature film was a Buck Jones western. Eugene paid attention at first, but then he began making soft moans, and soon louder moans. "My stomach hurts," he complained. And during a big Indian raid, Eugene got sick. It made him feel better, but it didn't do much for the Skelly gas station operator. Since he was responsible for the herd of kids, he had to help the theater management clean up. The manager provided him with a bucket and mop, while we

moved to another section of the theater to watch the further adventures of Buck Jones.

Eugene had no further incidents in the theater, but on the way out, he managed to find another nickel in his pocket and he bought himself a Schutter's Bit-O-Honey candy bar.

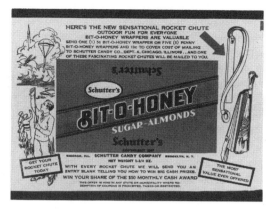

"Wow! Look at that," he exclaimed when he saw the wrapper. "You can get a rocket chute just by sending in this wrapper and ten cents!"

During the three-mile trip home, that's all Eugene babbled about. He had forgotten all about the Jimmie Allen Flying Club. And I had a sneaking suspicion that the Skelly gas station operator was counting his blessings. By the time he got us all back to the gas station, he undoubtedly felt as if he had just been released from an engagement in the lion's cage.

Soon everyone wanted a collection of Bit-O-Honey rocket chutes. The contraptions consisted of a slingshot that propelled a folded chute that opened on descent. I got mine by sending in five one-cent wrappers and a dime. Eugene got his with a nickel wrapper, and he soon became proficient at launching his rocket to what seemed like incredible heights.

Soon Eugene organized a rocket contest, in which all kids could participate—even kids from other neighborhoods—and he convinced Catharine's Uncle Ted to be the judge. Uncle Ted decided to hold the contest near a house so he'd have a roof line to use as a measurement.

As luck would have it, the best house was the double-decker in which Eugene lived. Uncle Ted figured its roof was high enough for the fifty or more feet the rocket chutes would achieve.

The day of the contest was sunny, but windy. Soon the sky was filled with ascending rocket chutes and descending parachutes. One of the adults in the neighborhood, Mr. DeRosa, was tending his vegetable garden and thought the Italian air force had come to take him back to the old country. The display in the sky was indeed impressive.

Uncle Ted fared a bit better than the Skelly gas station operator. He could yell louder than any of us kids, so he'd bellow out directions. Each of us got two turns, and after an hour or so the contest had narrowed down to three finalists. One of them was Eugene.

The other two final contestants took their turns. Then Eugene put everything he had into his slingshot and winged that rocket chute into the sky. We could tell immediately that Eugene would be the victor. When the chute cleared the chimney, Uncle Ted shouted, "Eugene's the winner and champ!"

On the descent, Eugene's chute opened but was caught in a gust of wind. The chute drifted over the roof and made a three-point landing in the leafy top of a gigantic red oak tree on the other side of the house.

Everyone "oohed" and "aahed." Except Eugene. He muttered one of those unprintable expressions that all of us kids knew even though our parents thought we didn't.

Everyone congratulated Eugene, and he acknowledged each one with a sad smile. I was the last to shake his hand and then I hurried home to catch the latest episode of Jimmie Allen. At the end of the program, a new premium offer was made. It sounded like one Eugene would enjoy, so I hurried back to his house after the program was over.

His mom answered the door. "You want Eugene, maybe? Well, he isn't home. But it's time for him to get his knickers in here!"

She stepped outside and hollered, "Eugene! Eugene!"

The answer was faint and far away, coming from the top of the big red oak. "I'm up here. I got my rocket chute, but now I'm afraid to climb down."

To make a long story short, the fire department came with their ladders. Since it was dark, lots of lights were flashed up into the tree so Eugene could be rescued.

Eugene's dad patted the firemen on the back for their efforts. And he patted Eugene a few times lower down to let him know that his rocket efforts really weren't scientific endeavors.

Eugene learned his lesson. From that day forward, he never had another Bit-O-Honey candy bar, nor was he ever known to crave Milk Duds again.

Moose, Not Mousse

When you think of confectionery products, you might envision a mousse, but not a moose. A moose belongs in the woods, or perhaps on the TV screen.

Bullwinkle J. Moose had his own TV program, "The Bullwinkle Show." It aired in prime time on NBC in 1961 and 1962. For the next two years, it was shown on Sunday afternoons and then Saturday mornings. Since then, Bullwinkle has appeared on various TV programs, still capturing the hearts of all who have a fondness for clever satire.

A candy bar, Bullwinkle's Nutty As a Fruit Cake, was manufactured during the mid to late 1970s by Carolyn's Candies, Inc., of Los Angeles, California. When Carolyn's Candies was taken over by Nellson's Candies, Inc., of Santa Monica, the Bullwinkle bar was dropped, sorry to say. It contained raisins, dates, peanuts, various other ingredients, and had a carob coating.

The drawing of Bullwinkle on the wrapper spoofed the centerfold that Burt Reynold's posed for in a women's magazine. The legend, "Eat Your Heart Out, Burt Reynolds!" didn't appear on the wrapper, but did appear on a souvenir Bullwinkle full-color poster that was suitable for framing.

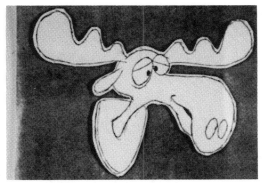

Jay Ward, Bullwinkle's daddy, became producer of animated films by accident. He had intended to be a real estate salesman and in 1947 opened an office in Oakland, California. A day later, a runaway truck smashed through the window of the office and broke Ward's leg. After a six-month stay in a plaster cast, Ward's thought roamed to professions other than sales. With an old friend, Alex Anderson, Ward decided to develop the animated cartoon, "Crusader Rabbit."

The venture was ahead of its time as far as television was concerned, but it did manage to run two years on NBC and then was syndicated for another twelve years.

In 1957, Ward met Bill Scott. Scott had collaborated on two prized Warner Brothers cartoons, "Mr. Magoo," and "Gerald McBoing-Boing." Ward and Scott formed Jay Ward Productions.

In the late 1950s, they produced "Rocky and His Friends," a limited-animation, half-hour show with real humor. It combined sharp comedy writing with general irreverence. In it, Rocky and Bullwinkle frequently talked back to the narrator. Rocky soon earned an audience among small fry and adults alike. "The Bullwinkle Show" carried on in the same tradition.

"The Bullwinkle Show" was basically a variety show, made up of different acts. Each show included Bullwinkle episodes. In Fractured Fairy Tales, a weekly episode, Edward Everett Horton narrated an old favorite. Horton also did the voice for Aesop in the Aesop and Son segment, which spoofed the fables. And in Peabody's Improbable History, historic events were treated with comedy rather than accuracy.

Bill Conrad's voice was also heard in various roles. Conrad had been the voice for Marshall Matt Dillon when "Gunsmoke" was a radio program. He later starred in "Cannon," a popular TV program that ran from 1971 to 1975.

Other popular features and characters on "The Bullwinkle Show" were the villains Natasha and Boris, and that great take-off on the Nelson Eddy image of the Canadian Royal Mounties, Dudley DoRight. Dudley cavorted with his horse, named simply Horse, and his lady friend, Nell Fenwick. To spice up the show, Snidely Whiplash appeared as the villain.

Over the years, Ward and Scott developed other TV cartoon features such as "Hoppity Hooper" in 1964 and "George of the Jungle" in 1968. The latter was Ward's last TV show, and as far as TV cartoons go, no one has yet come close to the track record for humor established by Ward.

Ward and company did produce commercials later on. The Cap'n Crunch commercials produced for Quaker Oats made that cereal a best seller for years.

Jay Ward, a truly creative personality (as well as a candy bar advocate), freaks out when candy bars are mentioned. When posed with the question, "If stuck on a desert isle alone with just one candy bar," he instantly chose Hershey's Golden Almond Bar.

While it was still on the market, the Bullwinkle bar was one of Ward's favorites. After all, he was Bullwinkle's daddy and was certainly sorry to see that bar go down the tubes. While it was around, it was sold at a nifty store called Dudley DoRight's Emporium in Hollywood. Still in operation, the Emporium carries all kinds of Bullwinkle/Rocky/Dudley items that fans can purchase as memorabilia.

Fergus and E.T.

You probably remember E.T., that lovable space creature who followed a candy trail laid down by Elliott, the young lad in the movie *E.T. the Extra-Terrestrial* (1982). Now, meet Fergus. She's a left-pawed dog with a hankering for candy (anything but licorice). And if anyone is E.T.'s counterpart on earth, Fergus is the one.

E.T. the Extra-Terrestrial was one of the all-time box office hits. But before the movie was produced, the M&M/Mars people weren't convinced E.T. would go over with the public. In the original movie script (and later in the book based on that script), M&M's were used to make the candy trail. But when the M&M/Mars people were asked if they'd like to tie into the movie, they said, "No." (Reliable information has it that M&M/Mars turned down the offer because they had recently been burned in a tie-in with another movie that had bombed at the box office.)

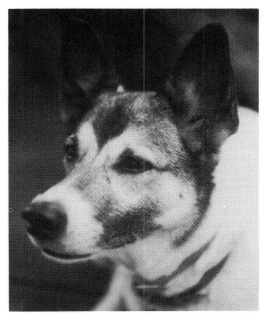

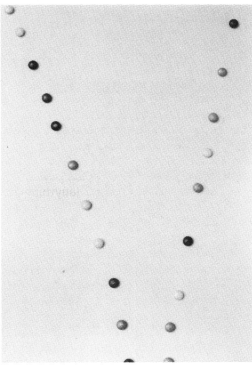

When M&M/Mars rejected the offer, the Hershey people quickly snapped up the opportunity to feature their Reese's Pieces in the candy trail. The rest is history. The movie became a smash hit, and Hershey turned out Reese's Pieces twenty-four hours a day in response to its overnight success.

E.T., then, really ate two different candy trails—one in the script/book, and one in the movie. One was of M&M's, the other of Reese's Pieces. Now suppose E.T. were real and he came back to earth. If there were two candy trails to follow, which one would he choose? The M&M's or the Reese's Pieces?

To find the answer to this serious question, we enlisted the services of E.T.'s counterpart, Fergus, an extra-perceptionary canine. While Fergus was snoozing under the dining room table, two trails were laid from the kitchen doorway into the living room. They began at the same point, but the trails veered off in opposite directions—the M&M's to the left, the Reese's Pieces to the right.

After the trails were laid, Fergus was awakened and led to the kitchen doorway starting point. Being a candy connoisseur, Fergus first sniffed and then crunched up a Reese's Piece. Then she went over to the M&M's trial and sniffed and crunched up an M&M. Now came the real test. Which "path" would she choose? Fergus went back to the Reese's Pieces trail and followed it to the end, gobbling up each and every one! Reese's Pieces was declared the winner!

Besides proving Reese's Pieces' appeal, the experiment also proved that Fergus is no one's fool. After a reasonable pause (a second-and-a-half) she did the only sensible thing a candy connoisseur could do. She galloped to the other trail and finished off all the M&M's.

Sweet Teaching

San Francisco teacher Gloria Maria Rando found a sweet way to teach reading to her first and second graders, for whom English is a second language. She uses a candy bar alphabet chart, a candy bar coloring book, and a jelly bean color chart with her grade-school youngsters.

"They pick a jelly bean out of the bag, identify the color orally, then read the correct color sentence aloud," she said. Color identification sentences are on a chart, and as a reward for proper identification, the student is given the chosen jelly bean.

On her candy bar alphabet chart, Gloria Maria has pasted various candy bar wrappers and boxes. Under each one is the first letter of the candy's name in both upper and lower cases. Included are such candy items as Almond Joy (Aa), Baby Ruth (Bb), Good and Plenty (Gg), Hot Tamales (Hh), Licorice Whips (Ll), M&M's (Mm), No Jelly (Nn), Oh Henry! (Oo), Planter (Pp), Rocky Road (Rr), U-No (Uu), and Zagnut (Zz).

You may be wondering what candy bar starts with the letter X. Well, Gloria Maria didn't find one, so she simply took two candy canes and crossed one over the other to make an X. Creative thinking comes naturally to this gifted teacher.

Where Are You?

You come to the corner of Cocoa Avenue and East Chocolate Avenue and make a left turn to Candy Lane. With

another left turn you're on 5th Avenue, eventually coming to Twizzlers Way. Where would you be? In an imaginary place, because the tour incorporates four different cities and towns that are the homes of confectioners.

Cocoa Avenue and Chocolate Avenue are in Hershey, Pennsylvania, home of the Hershey Chocolate Company. You'll find the Howard B. Stark Company on Candy Lane in Pewaukee, Wisconsin. Luden's, Inc. are headquartered in Reading, Pennsylvania. When that company celebrated its one-hundredth anniversary, the town of Reading honored it by naming a street for Luden's famous candy bar, 5th Avenue.

And to find Twizzlers Way, you'll have to go all the way to Farmington, New Mexico, home of the Y & S Candies plant.

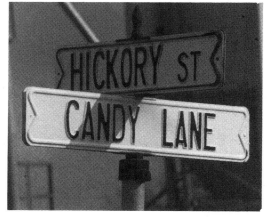

Desert Isles and Candy Bars

Suppose you were stuck alone on a desert isle with just one candy bar. What would you want that candy bar to be? That question was posed to various per-

sonalities, and their responses were sometimes humorous, sometimes right to the point, and sometimes they avoided answering the question entirely.

Rudy Vallee

The radio craze that swept America in the 1920s introduced Rudy Vallee and his megaphone. Listeners sat entranced as they listened to Rudy croon such hits as "My Time is Your Time," "Maine Stein Song," and the song that gave him his nickname, "I'm Just a Vagabond Lover." Vallee went on to many successes in later years, both in the movies and on stage.

In response to the desert island question, Rudy Vallee replied, "On that isle I would enjoy. . .the candy bar. . .advertised on TV showing the chocolate being poured over the coconut. . .a Mounds candy bar. In fact, I'd appreciate a few from the Mounds company!"

Valee also said that in the early 1930s, a Rudy Vallee candy bar was produced for a short while. As Vallee recollected, the bar didn't sell well, so was dropped from the market. The company that manufactured the bar was located in Maine, so perhaps the company owner felt the urge to go moose hunting rather

than continue making the Rudy Vallee bar. No one will ever know.

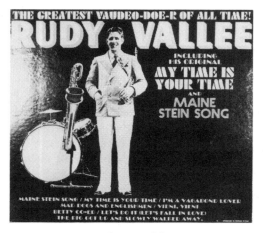

John Updike
John Updike is one of America's finest writers and has been known to nibble on a candy bar while crafting a story. His response to the desert isle question was "One candy bar per desert isle? That's a touch choice, but I think, after a longing look at a Reese's Peanut Butter Cup (crunchy style), I'll have to opt for a classic Milky Way, Fresh from a refrigerator, though, and not all melted together."

Updike is not alone when it comes to Milky Way madness. Mimi Sheraton, who wrote eloquently on restaurants and food for the *New York Times*, confessed in one of her columns that every so often a longing for a frozen Milky Way swept over her. When that happened, the only solution was to freeze one and eat it. Sheraton cautioned that there was a definite knack to biting into a frozen Milky Way. You had to attack the bar at a corner and work gradually toward the center using the canine and side teeth.

John MacDonald
A marvelous writer, John D. MacDonald is the author of many short stories and novels. He's best known for his series character, Travis McGee, who appears in a shelfull of hard-to-put-down novels.

His response to being stuck with just one candy bar on a desert isle is "Stuck with just one candy bar? Then it would

have to be Cadbury's Coffee Mocha, which loving grandchildren send me from New Zealand when I can't buy them here.

"My second choice would have to be Candy Barr, one of the more skillful strippers of this century."

Donald E. Westlake
Perhaps the funniest mystery writer around today, Donald Westlake has a zany sense of humor that comes across in the adventures of the bumbling Dortmunder gang. He has a more serious side when he writes mysteries under the names of Richard Stark or Tucker Coe.

Westlake's response to the question was, "My first reaction to your question was to say, 'If I were stuck alone on a desert isle with just one candy bar, I would like that candy bar to be Candy Barr.' But then it occurred to me almost any mature adult would give you that answer, so then I decided that just any Bit-O-Honey would do. But that suggested a certain immaturity on my part, so finally I decided if I were stuck alone on a desert isle with just one candy bar, I would like it to be a candy bar with a radio transmitter in it!"

BIT-O-HONEY®

Candy Barr
Candy Barr was the stage name of Juanita Dale Phillips. Trying to track her down was an experience in itself. First contacted was *G-String Beat*, a periodical from Gays Mills, Wisconsin, Box 007. Rita Atlanta, who was connected with that periodical and also was the overseas representative of the Continental Theatrical Agency, was most helpful in providing the name of a person who would know where Candy Barr might be. Next contacted was Jennie Lee, president of the Exotic Dancers League in San Pedro, California.

She provided an address. Unfortunately, efforts to establish communications with Ms. Barr were unsuccessful. Nevertheless, Ray Broekel, John D. MacDonald, and Donald Westlake, all being mature adults, wish her well wherever she might be.

Joan Lowery Nixon

A fine writer of mysteries for young readers, Nixon offered a well-plotted answer. "Since your 'set up' is improbable, I assume you want lightweight answers, so. . .The candy bar I would choose to have with me on a desert island would be 3 Musketeers, since the Three Musketeers' ability to get out of tight spots is legendary. I assume that if they found a way to escape the desert island they'd take me with them. A second choice would be a Snickers. A good laugh helps out any bad situation."

Mary Blount Christian

Another fine writer of books for children, Christian responds in this fashion: "If I were stranded on a desert island I suppose I'd long for the candy of my youth, a Bit-O-Honey, because I could make one of those last through a double feature and five cartoons and a serial episode on a Saturday at the movies, or through a Nancy Drew or Brenda Starr mystery, and one ought to last until the rescue ship comes. (Actually I'd throw away the candy and settle for Paul Newman or Pierce Brosnan!)

Isaac Asimov

What an author this man is! He's skilled in all kinds of writing but is perhaps best known for his science fiction. His clever answer to the question was, "On a desert island, I would want a whopper of a bittersweet chocolate bar with almonds—with the added property of being able to grow back any piece that was bitten off."

Ben Bova

Another premier science fiction writer and former editor of *Astounding Science Fiction* and *Omni*, Bova replied, "I'm not much of a candy bar eater. Used to be, back when they were made with real chocolate, and a nickel would buy you a good-sized handful of candy. . . . Being of Italian extraction, if I were stuck on a desert isle I would much rather have a large pizza (extra sauce and cheese, nothing else on it) than any candy bar."

Billy Graham

Billy Graham, evangelist, is known worldwide and had a staff member, Shirley A. Miller, respond to the question. "Since Mr. Graham is away from the office so much of the time due to his extensive travels and many speaking engagements, we are unable to provide you with the information you want. . . . May God bless you."

Jerry Falwell

Jerry Falwell, head of The Old-Time Gospel Hour, also had a staff member respond to the question. Steven Scott said, "We are grateful for your kind offer but we are unable to take advantage of your suggestion. It is our prayer that the Lord will meet all your needs and guide you in His perfect will. Sincerely in Christ."

Seymour Reit

A well-known author of books for both adults and children, Reit has another distinction. He was the father of Casper the Friendly Ghost. Reit created the character and wrote the first Casper story, which was used word for word as the voice-over narration for the first Casper film in the early 1940s. It won an Oscar nomination, and on that basis Fleisher Studios launched a Casper series. Along came TV, and the rest is history.

Reit, never one to bandy words, responded: 'Re your question—there's only *one* candy bar for a desert island: the biggest damn one you can find!"

Friendly phantom . . .

Dorothy B. Hughes

One of the premier mystery writers of all time, Hughes responded to the question from London, England. "I'd much rather have a tomato on my desert isle. But if I have to take a chocolate bar, I've decided I'll take a Cadbury's Fruit and Nut—a nice fresh one like we get in England, not those stale ones they ship to us in the U.S.

"And if it's a great American candy bar you require, I'll take the Hershey bar I had every week when I was a little girl. They were enormous and cost five cents and had only the best ingredients."

William Manchester

His books have chronicled the lives of John F. Kennedy, Douglas MacArthur, and H. L. Mencken, among others. He replied, "If I were alone on a desert island, the candy bar I would choose would be a Butterfinger. I became addicted to Butterfingers as a boy, and while I rarely eat candy now, if I do that's my choice."

Verne N. Rockcastle

A professor of science and environmental education and a jogger of renown, Rockcastle answered, "What bar I'd like to have if stuck on a desert isle...it would be Mr. Goodbar in a giant size. I'd put that first because I like the crisp combination of chocolate, nuts, etc. That's assuming, of course, that I couldn't get the Hershey Golden Almond."

Robert Hayden

Prominent educator and author, Hayden chooses "Old Nick—because it was yummy and chewy and I remember it as my first and favorite bar as a youngster of five."

Bill Pronzini

Another top-notch mystery novel writer, Pronzini replied, "If I were stuck on a desert isle with just one candy bar, what would I like that candy bar to be? Well, let's see. Would Milk Duds qualify as a candy bar? They were always my favorite as a kid, and of course I could ration them one per day on the island, for survival purposes. If Milk Duds don't qualify, I suppose I'll have to go with 3 Musketeers—mainly because I've never cared much for peanuts in my candy. A third choice would be that unsung but delicious bar, Charleston Chew."

Jack Ritchie

Recently passed away, Jack Ritchie was one of the finest mystery short story writers in recent times. Ritchie replied to the question in a most imaginative way, "Well, it all depends. . . . If I had to go as I am now, it would have to be a Milky Way bar. Large size. I like the chocolate covering and that streak of caramel inside. And it melts in your mouth. It doesn't have to be chewed or crunched.

"But on the other hand, if I could go to that island with a full set of sound teeth (and if we can imagine a desert island, why can't we imagine sound teeth?), my choice would be a Baby Ruth bar. Absolutely delicious. Chocolate, caramel, *and* peanuts. Which I could chew and crunch. Heaven.

"While I'm at it, couldn't we put a few trees on that desert isle? Perhaps a little hut? A small garden? With a few measly peanut plants? A couple of cacao trees? Some sugar cane? (I forget to tell you that *my* desert island has a little oasis on one end where you can grow sugar cane.) Maybe I could manufacture my own Baby Ruths? I'm willing to give it a try."

Thomas G. Aylesworth

Raconteur, world traveler, writer, and editor, Aylesworth replied, "If I were stuck alone on a desert isle with just one candy bar, I might make it a 3 Musketeers (they are good, and can fill you up, but I wish they still came in three sections). However, if we are talking about sensual gustatory delirium, I would choose a Heath Bar, biting off a bit, letting the chocolate melt and ooze down my throat, and then

chewing the delicious toffee inside. I can make one of those last all day."

Patty Wolcott Berger

Patty Wolcott is the author of many well-known children's books that each contain only ten different words. Her husband, Raoul Berger, is a distinguished scholar and authority on the Constitution. Mrs. Berger replied, "Raoul feels it wouldn't be appropriate for an eighty-two-year-old man to wax lyrical about a candy bar. My ten-word-line for you is this: I would want a bar of bittersweet chocolate for solace."

Tomie dePaola

A writer and illustrator of children's books, dePaola had an assistant, Robert Allan Hechtel, reply. "In answer to your question regarding candy bars, Tomie dePaola would say, 'If I were stuck alone on a desert isle with just one candy bar, I'd want that candy bar to be a Snickers.' "

Ed Emberly

Another master at writing and illustrating children's books, Emberley couldn't resist adding illustrations to both his response and the envelope. His word answer said, "A chocolate-covered Friendship Sloop—30' overall—milk or dark—diesel power preferred—nuts (almond or hazel) optional."

Gregory Mcdonald

Greg Mcdonald is the author of many good mysteries, including ones with that wild and woolly adventurer, Fletch. Mcdonald's reply to the question is a study in well-chosen words. "The first of many times I have been stuck literally on a desert isle, I was a lad in Canada most keen on the Cadbury Caramello Bar. It is good to be literally stuck young. It fixes one's initial cravings, imbues them with a certain innocence.

"Over subsequent incidents of my being literally stuck on desert isles, my subsequent cravings became more mature, possibly more sinister. Consider the baked bean. Nevertheless, my initial craving, even when only figuratively stuck on a desert isle, now, remains the Cadbury Caramello. From this you may take it that I believe cravings develop and express themselves ontologically. Figuratively stuck on desert isles frequently now in fact (although I never expected to have to admit this publically), I have a drawer in my study kept filled with Cadbury Caramello Bars."

Art Buchwald and Gloria Steinem

What a great way to end this survey—by pairing Art Buchwald and Gloria Steinem. Not only are they well-known public figures, they both also supplied short answers to the question.

Steinem responded, "I'm not sure it's worth a sentence, but Heath Bars are my favorite."

And Buchwald leaves us three words to contemplate and crunch upon. "A granola bar."

So it goes with desert isles, candy bars (or lack of), and personalities. What about you? What would your choice be? If you're a mature adult male, how would you spell "bar"?

Candy Bar Wrappers

Recommended Price List

The following list establishes reasonable prices for candy bar wrappers, allowing for collector variables.

Category I

These are base prices for wrappers with conventional art or just the names, plus other printing.

Condition	Mint/ Excellent	Slightly Worn	Worn/ Tears
Pre-1920s	$10 +	$9 +	$8 +
1920s	5 +	4 +	3 +
1930s	4 +	3 +	2 +
1940s	3 +	2 +	1 +
1950s	2 +	1.50 +	.75
1960s	1 +	.75	.50
1970s	.75	.50	.50 –
1980s	.50	.50 –	.50 –

Category II

These are additional prices that can be added to base prices listed above for wrappers with special art designs.

Pre-1920s through 1940s	$5 +
1950s to 1970s	$3 +

Category III

These additional prices can be added for wrappers with other special features or personalities.

Pre-1920s through 1940s	$5 +
1950s to 1970s	$3 +

A wrapper may fit in just Category I, in one additional category, or in all three categories. An example of a wrapper that qualifies in all three categories is the It bar. The It wrapper came out in the 1920s, contains special art designs, and represents a personality, Clara Bow, the It girl of the movies. Its value is around $20 if it is in mint to excellent condition.

The 1930s Dick Tracy wrapper fits Category I and Category III and is worth about $9 if in mint to excellent condition. The 1940s Giant bar wrapper fits Category I and is worth around $3, mint to excellent.

Buy wrappers individually, if possible. If you're buying collections or pig-in-a-poke assortments, pay half or less the recommended prices listed above.

Candy bar wrapper condition definitions are as follows:

Mint/Excellent condition—Press wrapper, not used; or if off candy bar, wrapper has no scratches and is intact throughout.

Slightly Worn—Wrapper intact, only a few notable creases.

Worn/Tears—Candy bar removed, possibly corners missing or tears.

You can receive more information about candy bar wrappers from The Great American Candy Bar Club. Active members save wrappers that most people throw away. They receive a club newsletter, *Candy Bar Gazebo*, swap duplicate wrappers, and trade information about the candy bar business past and present.

Reproduced below is the club membership card, front and back. If you are interested in joining the club, simply send a self-addressed, stamped envelope to Ray Broekel, Six Edge Street, Ipswich, Massachusetts 01938.

Index

About the Author

Ray Broekel was born on a farm in Germany, raised in Illinois, and married in Texas. He and his wife Peg have also lived in South Carolina, California, Connecticut, and Massachusetts. Besides teaching, Ray has been in the writing and publishing business for more than forty years. The author of more than fifteen-hundred stories and articles and more than one-hundred-fifty books for children, his *Great American Candy Bar Book* was published in 1982.

That book earned him the reputation as the number one authority on American candy bar history. Now a featured columnist for two magazines, he's also the editor of the newsletter *Candy Bar Gazebo*.

Broekel has a large collection of candy bar memorabilia, including thousands of old and new candy bar wrappers. The wrapper collection is still growing.